I0415659

July 2012

OIL AND GAS MANAGEMENT

Interior's Reorganization Complete, but Challenges Remain in Implementing New Requirements

GAO

Accountability ★ Integrity ★ Reliability

GAO-12-423

July 2012

G A O
Accountability * Integrity * Reliability
Highlights

Highlights of GAO-12-423, a report to congressional requesters

OIL AND GAS MANAGEMENT

Interior's Reorganization Complete, but Challenges Remain in Implementing New Requirements

Why GAO Did This Study

On April 20, 2010, the *Deepwater Horizon* drilling rig exploded in the Gulf of Mexico resulting in 11 deaths, serious injuries, and the largest marine oil spill in U.S. history. Interior, which oversees offshore oil and gas activities, initiated a number of reforms following the incident to improve its oversight. This report assesses (1) Interior's reorganization of its oversight of offshore oil and gas activities; (2) how key policy changes Interior has implemented since this incident have affected Interior's environmental analyses, plan reviews, and drilling permit reviews; (3) the extent to which Interior's inspections of drilling rigs and production platforms in the Gulf identify violations or result in civil penalty assessments; (4) when stakeholders provided input to Interior on proposed oil and gas activities, and the extent which they believe Interior considered their concerns; and (5) key challenges, if any, Interior faces in overseeing offshore oil and gas activities in the Gulf. GAO analyzed data and documents and interviewed officials from Interior and the Department of Commerce's National Oceanic and Atmospheric Administration, Gulf of Mexico states, environmental groups, and industry.

What GAO Recommends

GAO recommends, among other things, that Interior improve the effectiveness of its inspections through timely input of violation correction data, its capacity for categorizing oil and gas activities according to risk, and its strategic planning for information technology and workforce efforts. In commenting on a draft of this report, Interior generally agreed with GAO's findings and recommendations.

View GAO-12-423. For more information, contact Frank Rusco at (202) 512-3841 or ruscof@gao.gov.

What GAO Found

On October 1, 2011, the Department of the Interior (Interior) officially established two new bureaus, separating offshore resource management oversight activities, such as reviewing oil and gas exploration and development plans, from safety and environmental oversight activities, such as reviewing drilling permits and inspecting drilling rigs. Because the responsibilities of these bureaus are closely interconnected and will depend on effective coordination, Interior developed memoranda and standard operating procedures to define roles and responsibilities and facilitate and formalize coordination.

New safety and environmental requirements and policy changes designed to mitigate the risk of a well blowout or spill initially required Interior to devote additional resources and time to reviewing certain oil and gas exploration and development plans and drilling permits for oil and gas activities in the Gulf of Mexico. Specifically, these policy changes affected Interior's (1) environmental analyses, (2) reviews of oil and gas exploration and development plans, and (3) reviews of oil and gas drilling permits.

Interior's inspections of offshore Gulf of Mexico oil and gas drilling rigs and production platforms from January 1, 2000, through September 30, 2011, routinely identified violations. However, Interior's database is missing data on when violations were identified as well as violation correction dates for about half of the violations issued. As a result, Interior does not know on a real-time basis whether or when all violations were identified and corrected, potentially allowing unsafe conditions to continue for extended periods. During this same period, Interior issued approximately $18 million in civil penalty assessments. Recently, Interior began implementing a number of policy changes to improve both its inspection and civil penalty programs. However, Interior has not assessed how these changes would affect its ability to conduct monthly drilling rig inspections.

Federal government stakeholders told GAO that they generally provided most of their input on Interior's oil and gas development program early in the planning process and typically did not review or comment on oil and gas exploration and development plans or drilling permits. Federal and state stakeholders stated that Interior was generally responsive to their input on proposed offshore oil and gas activities in the Gulf of Mexico from 2002 through January 2012, but nongovernmental stakeholders—including industry and conservation groups—stated that Interior was, at times, less responsive.

Interior continues to face challenges following its reorganization that may affect its ability to oversee oil and gas activities in the Gulf of Mexico. Specifically, Interior's capacity to identify and evaluate risk remains limited, raising questions about the effectiveness with which it allocates its oversight resources. Interior also continues to experience difficulties in implementing effective information technology systems, such as those that aid exploration and development plan reviews. It also continues to face workforce planning challenges, including hiring, retaining, and training staff. Moreover, Interior does not have current strategic plans to guide its information technology or workforce planning efforts.

_____ **United States Government Accountability Office**

Contents

Tables

Figures

Abbreviations

API	American Petroleum Institute
BOEM	Bureau of Ocean Energy Management
BOEMRE	Bureau of Ocean Energy, Management, Regulation and Enforcement
BSEE	Bureau of Safety and Environmental Enforcement
EA	environmental assessment
EIS	environmental impact statement
FWS	Fish and Wildlife Service
GIS	geographic information system
IT	information technology
MOU	memorandum of understanding
MMS	Minerals Management Service
NEPA	National Environmental Policy Act of 1969, as amended
NOAA	National Oceanic and Atmospheric Administration
OCS	outer continental shelf
OCS Lands Act	Outer Continental Shelf Lands Act
TIMS	Technical Information Management System

July 30, 2012

The Honorable Sheldon Whitehouse
Chairman
Subcommittee on Oversight
Committee on Environment
   and Public Works
United States Senate

The Honorable Nick J. Rahall, II
House of Representatives

On April 20, 2010, the *Deepwater Horizon* drilling rig exploded in the Gulf of Mexico, resulting in 11 deaths, serious injuries, and the largest marine oil spill in the history of the United States. Located over 40 miles off the coast of Louisiana and at a depth of nearly 5,000 feet in the Gulf of Mexico, the subsea well spilled oil for 87 days before responders were able to cap the well and contain the flow of oil. According to government estimates, by that time, over 4.9 million barrels of oil had spilled into the Gulf of Mexico. In addition to the tragic loss of life, the explosion, fire, and catastrophic oil spill damaged the environment and resulted in a loss of livelihoods and harm to local economies, with estimated compensation costs totaling in the billions of dollars. Following this incident, the Department of the Interior (Interior)—which is responsible for overseeing oil and gas activities on federal lands and waters—initiated a number of policy reforms to strengthen its oversight of offshore oil and gas production on the outer continental shelf (OCS),[1] including in the Gulf of Mexico. While these reforms were being developed and implemented, Interior imposed a moratorium on certain offshore drilling operations that mainly affected deepwater oil and gas projects.[2]

Under the Outer Continental Shelf Lands Act (OCS Lands Act) of 1953, as amended,[3] Interior is responsible for leasing federal lands on the OCS

---

[1]The OCS refers to the submerged lands outside the territorial jurisdiction of all 50 states, but within U.S. jurisdiction and control. The portion of the North American continental edge that is federally designated as the OCS generally extends seaward 3 geographical miles off the coastline to at least 200 nautical miles.

[2]Interior considers deepwater projects to be in water depths of 500 feet or greater.

[3]43 U.S.C. §§ 1331-1356.

to meet the nation's energy needs and generate revenue for the federal government in a manner that protects the environment. Through its three OCS regional offices—in Alaska, the Gulf of Mexico, and the Pacific OCS regions, Interior manages more than 1.7 billion acres of the OCS, which, according to its estimates, may contain as much as 88.6 billion barrels of oil and 398.4 trillion cubic feet of natural gas.[4] Over the past 5 years, Interior has collected about $13 billion per year in royalties and other payments from companies utilizing public resources, including those producing oil and gas from offshore and onshore federal leases. This represents one of the largest nontax sources of federal government funds. While total domestic production of oil and gas had been on a slow decline and flat, respectively, for many years, recent innovations allowing new production from shale formations onshore, and increases in oil and gas production in deepwater areas of the Gulf of Mexico, have led to a reversal of that trend. Figures 1 and 2 illustrate trends in shallow water and deepwater Gulf of Mexico oil and gas production from 1990 through 2010—the last year complete data were available. While oil produced from shallow waters has been in decline since 1996, deepwater oil production has been increasing and was at an all-time high in 2010 (see fig. 1). In 2010, according to Interior, oil produced from offshore federal leases—which is almost at a 20-year high—accounted for approximately 29 percent of domestic production.

---

[4]Bureau of Ocean Energy Management. Assessment of Undiscovered Technically Recoverable Oil and Gas Resources of the National Outer Continental Shelf, 2011.

Figure 1: OCS Oil Production (in Thousands of Barrels), 1990 through 2010

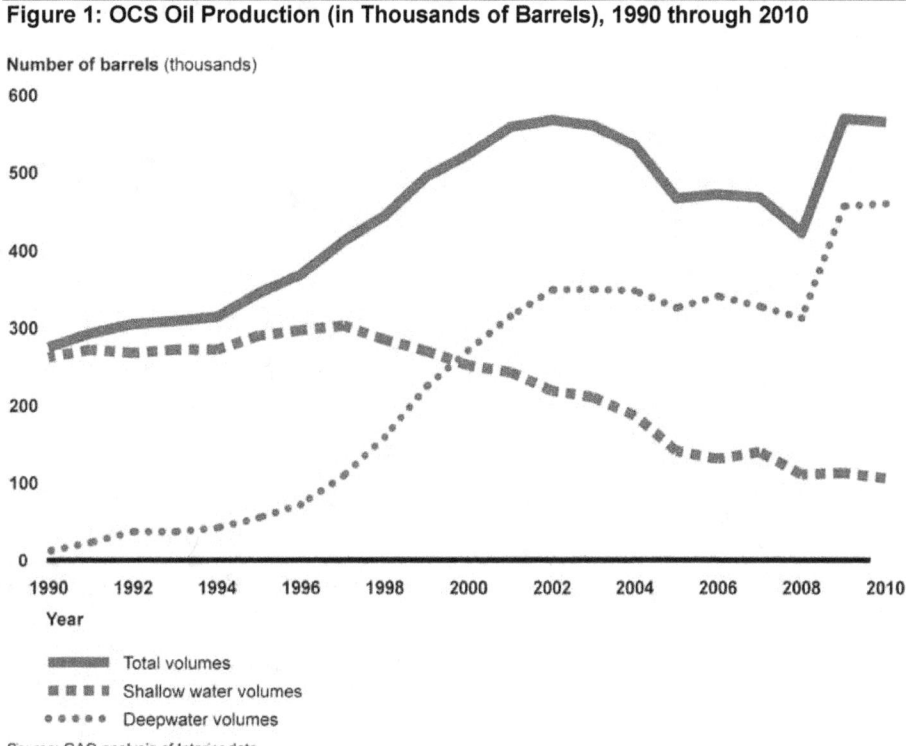

Source: GAO analysis of Interior data.

Unlike oil, total production of natural gas in the Gulf of Mexico has been in decline since around 2002. Specifically, shallow water gas production has been in decline since 1996, while deepwater gas increased through 2003 and then started to slightly decline (see fig. 2). This was generally mirrored by decreasing production onshore until recent years. The recent turnaround and growth in domestic gas production has been led by the development of gas in shale formations, which are largely on nonfederal lands. In 2010, according to Interior, natural gas produced from offshore federal leases accounted for approximately 10 percent of total production on federal leases and approximately 8 percent of total domestic production.

Figure 2: OCS Natural Gas Production (in Millions of Cubic Feet), 1990 through 2010

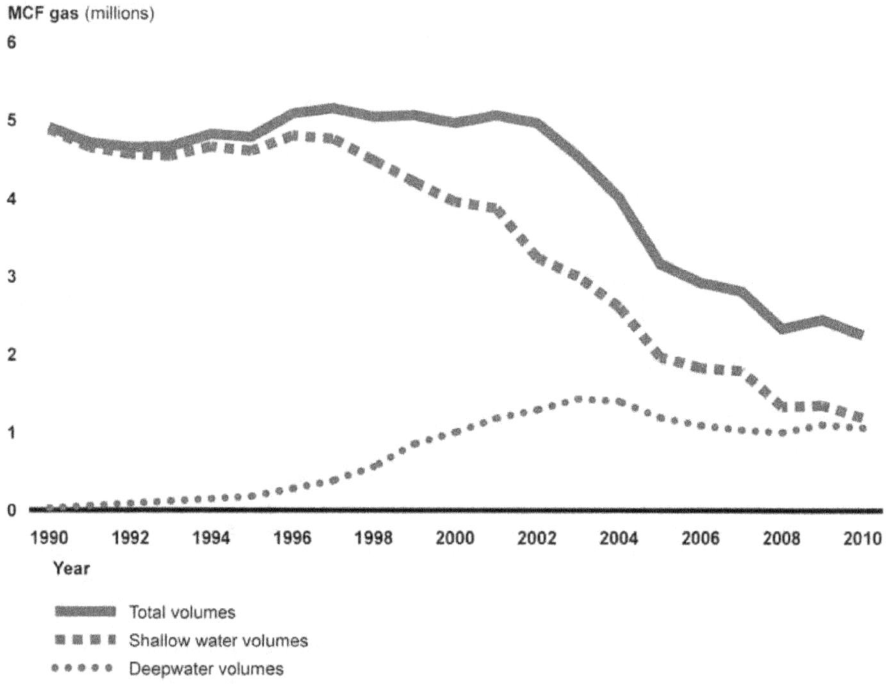

Source: GAO analysis of Interior data.

Interior's responsibilities for managing offshore oil and gas production activities include administering leases and reviewing and approving exploration and development plans as well as applications for drilling permits from operators—companies that develop the federal leases—and inspecting offshore drilling rigs and production platforms to ensure compliance with safety and environmental requirements. The *Deepwater Horizon* incident raised questions about Interior's oversight of offshore oil and gas activities in the Gulf of Mexico and led to a number of reviews—including those by the National Commission on the BP *Deepwater Horizon* Oil Spill and Offshore Drilling and Interior's Outer Continental Shelf Safety Oversight Board.[5] These reviews generated more than 200 recommendations to improve Interior's oversight. In May 2010, Interior

---

[5]The board was created by secretarial order to review and oversee Interior OCS operations to support reasoned and fact-based recommendations for potential improvement.

announced plans to significantly reorganize the bureau that managed oil and gas activities on the OCS and collected royalties. In February 2011, GAO added Interior's oversight of oil and gas resources to its list of programs at high risk of waste, fraud, abuse, and mismanagement or in need of broad reform, citing concerns about Interior's ability to undertake this reorganization while continuing to carry out its ongoing oversight responsibilities, weaknesses in its human capital management, and shortcomings in its revenue collection policies.[6]

You asked us to review Interior's oversight of offshore oil and gas activities in the Gulf of Mexico. Specifically, this report examines (1) Interior's reorganization of its oversight of offshore oil and gas activities in the Gulf of Mexico since the *Deepwater Horizon* incident; (2) how key policy changes Interior has implemented since this incident have affected Interior's National Environmental Policy Act (NEPA) analyses, plans reviews, and drilling permit reviews; (3) the extent to which Interior's inspections of Gulf of Mexico drilling rigs and production platforms identified violations or resulted in civil penalty assessments, and how key policy changes since this incident have affected Interior's inspection and civil penalties program; (4) when stakeholders have provided input to Interior about proposed offshore oil and gas activities, and the extent to which stakeholders believe Interior considered such input from approximately 2002 through January 2012; and (5) key challenges, if any, affecting Interior's oversight of offshore oil and gas activities in the Gulf of Mexico following its reorganization.

To conduct this work, we reviewed relevant laws and regulations and Interior documents, guidance, and data. We also interviewed officials in Interior's headquarters and Gulf of Mexico regional offices as well as officials from other federal agencies and state governments and representatives from industry and conservation groups. To identify actions Interior has taken as part of its reorganization efforts, we reviewed agency documentation and guidance and interviewed knowledgeable agency officials. Because the reorganization was not fully complete until October 1, 2011, we did not evaluate the effectiveness of the reorganization on Interior's ability to conduct oversight of oil and gas activities in the Gulf of Mexico. To examine Interior's processes and policy changes and their effects, we reviewed agency documents relevant

---

[6]GAO, *High Risk Series: An Update,* GAO-11-278 (Washington, D.C.: February 2011).

to Interior's work with the National Environmental Policy Act of 1969, as amended (NEPA),[7] exploration and development plans, and drilling permits. Because many of these policy changes are still under way and have not been in force long enough to evaluate, we did not evaluate the effectiveness of the policy changes to reduce the risk associated with offshore oil and gas activities in this report. We analyzed Interior data on its NEPA reviews and plan approvals from January 1, 2000, through September 30, 2011, and drilling permit approvals from January 1, 2005, through September 30, 2011, and interviewed knowledgeable Interior officials. To determine the extent to which Interior's inspections resulted in violations and civil penalty assessments, we analyzed Interior's inspection data from January 1, 2000, through September 30, 2011. We assessed the reliability of these data by (1) reviewing documentation about the data and the system that produced them, (2) interviewing agency officials knowledgeable about the data, and (3) verifying our results with agency officials. Based on this assessment, we found these data sufficiently reliable for our purposes. To determine the extent to which Interior considered and addressed stakeholder concerns, we reviewed relevant laws and interviewed stakeholders, including officials from the Department of Commerce's National Oceanic and Atmospheric Administration (NOAA); Interior's Fish and Wildlife Service (FWS); the five Gulf of Mexico states (Alabama, Florida, Louisiana, Mississippi, and Texas); and representatives from selected nongovernmental organizations, including conservation and industry groups.[8] To identify challenges Interior faces, we reviewed relevant law and agency documentation and guidance and interviewed knowledgeable agency officials. While Interior is also responsible for overseeing offshore oil and gas activities in all federal waters of the United States, the vast majority of such activities currently take place in the Gulf of Mexico and, therefore, we focused our review on activities in the Gulf of Mexico. Additional details on our scope and methodology can be found in appendix I.

---

[7]Pub. L. No. 91-190, 83 Stat. 852 (1970), codified as amended at 42 U.S.C. §§ 4321-4347 (2011). Under NEPA, federal agencies must assess the effects of major federal actions—those they propose to carry out or to permit—that significantly affect the environment.

[8]Conservation organizations were selected based on the following criteria: (1) they were involved in environmental issues specific to the Gulf of Mexico, (2) they were referred to us by a representative from a conservation group that we initially interviewed, and (3) time and resource constraints.

We conducted this performance audit from September 2010 to July 2012 in accordance with generally accepted government auditing standards. Those standards require that we plan and perform the audit to obtain sufficient, appropriate evidence to provide a reasonable basis for our findings and conclusions based on our audit objectives. We believe that the evidence obtained provides a reasonable basis for our findings and conclusions based on our audit objectives.

Background

This section provides a history of Interior's oversight of oil and gas resources, a summary of the oil and gas development process in the Gulf of Mexico, and a brief timeline of key events since the *Deepwater Horizon* incident.

History of Interior's Oversight of Oil and Gas Resources

Interior was created by Congress in 1849, and part of Interior's mission is to oversee the nation's publicly owned natural resources, including parks, wildlife habitat, and oil and natural gas resources on millions of acres onshore and offshore in OCS waters. With regard to oil and gas resources in particular, Interior leases federal lands and submerged lands on the OCS to oil and gas companies, issues permits for oil and gas drilling to operators, and conducts inspections of such drilling and production operations. In 1982, by secretarial order, the Secretary of the Interior created the Minerals Management Service (MMS), consolidating all of Interior's OCS minerals responsibilities into a single agency. This secretarial order gave MMS the authority to assess the nature, extent, recoverability, and value of leasable minerals on the OCS. To manage OCS energy resources, the Offshore Energy and Minerals Management program within MMS carried out resource evaluations and classifications, environmental studies and reviews, lease sales and management, and inspection and enforcement activities. Until June 2010, this program oversaw a number of scientific and technical research efforts and funded scientific studies that contributed to understanding the potential effects of OCS operations on human, marine, and coastal environments. MMS's Minerals Revenue Management program conducted oversight of royalty payments paid by companies on the production of oil and gas from federal leases.

We and others, including Interior's Office of Inspector General, have reported on a history of problems with Interior's management of oil and gas resources.[9,10] In 2010, shortly after the *Deepwater Horizon* incident, Interior announced that it would reorganize its offshore oversight and revenue collection functions. Specifically, Interior renamed MMS the Bureau of Ocean Energy, Management, Regulation and Enforcement (BOEMRE) as an interim step before eventually restructuring it into three separate bureaus—the Bureau of Ocean Energy Management (BOEM), responsible for leasing and resource management; the Bureau of Safety and Environmental Enforcement (BSEE), responsible for issuing oil and natural gas drilling permits and conducting inspections; and the Office of Natural Resources Revenue, responsible for revenue collection.[11] Within the Gulf of Mexico region, BOEM and BSEE each have a regional office in New Orleans, and BSEE has five additional district offices located in southern Louisiana and Texas that report to the BSEE regional office (see fig. 3). For leasing purposes, the Gulf of Mexico is composed of three geographic planning areas—eastern, central, and western.

---

[9]GAO, *Oil and Gas Management: Interior's Oil and Gas Production Verification Efforts Do Not Provide Reasonable Assurance of Accurate Measurement of Production Volumes*, GAO-10-313 (Washington, D.C.: Mar. 15, 2010).

[10]DOI OIG, *Minerals Management Service: Royalty-in-Kind Program's Oil Verification Process*, C-IN-MMS-0007-2008 (Washington, D.C.: May 2010).

[11]This report focuses on BOEM and BSEE; it does not examine the Office of Natural Resources Revenue.

Figure 3: BOEM and BSEE Regional Offices and BSEE District Offices in the Gulf of Mexico (2012)

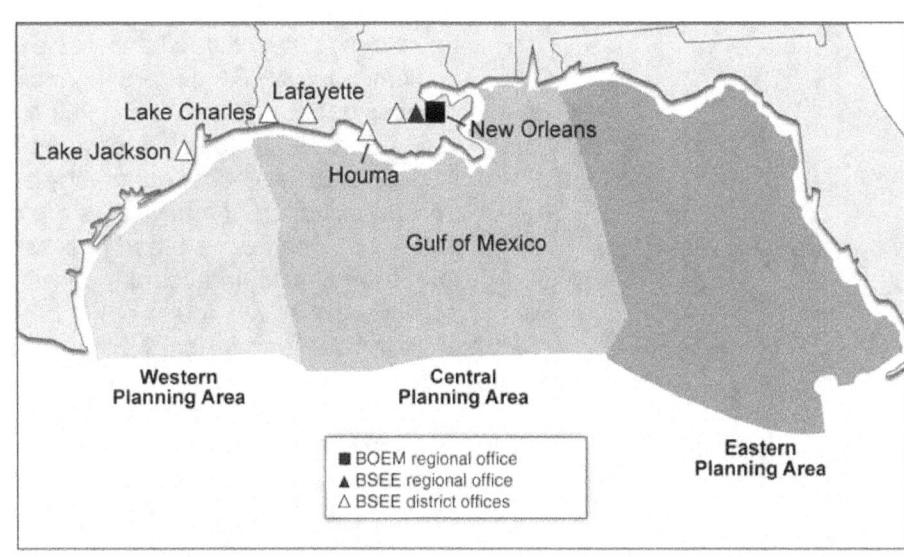

Sources: Interior documentation and Map Resources (map).

Oil and Gas Development in the Gulf of Mexico

In planning and managing offshore oil and gas development to meet its requirements under federal law, Interior follows a complex process combining resource development with assessments of potential environmental and cultural effects. Throughout this process, Interior must meet the federal requirements articulated in the OCS Lands Act while also complying with NEPA and other laws that require the consideration of the potential effects of offshore oil and gas development on environmental and cultural resources. Under NEPA, all federal agencies are to evaluate the likely environmental effects of actions they propose to carry out or permit. NEPA has two principal purposes: (1) to ensure that an agency carefully considers detailed information concerning significant environmental effects and (2) to ensure that this information will be made available to the public. Under NEPA, before initiating any oil and gas planning, leasing, exploration, or development activities, Interior must evaluate likely environmental effects of those activities. Generally, the scope of those activities requires Interior to use either an environmental assessment (EA)—a concise analysis developed if the environmental effect of the proposed action is unknown or has the potential to be significant—or, if the action is likely to affect the environment significantly, a more detailed environmental impact statement (EIS). EIS regulations include multiple opportunities for public comment—including commenting on the draft EIS—and require plans for mitigating adverse effects. EA and EIS documents are intended to help decision makers understand the environmental consequences associated with proposed activities, such as those associated with oil and gas exploration and development. In implementing NEPA, federal agencies may rely on a "tiering" process—a process generally sanctioned in the governing regulations for NEPA, in which prior NEPA reviews, such as EIS or EA documents, are incorporated into subsequent, site-specific analyses. Tiering is used to avoid duplication of analysis as a proposed activity moves through the NEPA process from a broad assessment to a site-specific analysis. Interior may also, in accordance with NEPA, categorically exclude activities previously found not to have a significant effect on the environment from further NEPA review.

Interior's process for the development of federal oil and gas resources in the Gulf of Mexico consists of the following stages: (1) preparing a nationwide 5-year oil and gas leasing program, (2) planning for and holding specific lease sales, (3) approving an operator's exploration plan, (4) approving an operator's development plan,[12] (5) approving an operator's drilling permit, and (6) inspecting offshore oil and gas activities.[13,14]

Stage 1: Preparing a nationwide 5-year oil and gas leasing program. Every 5 years, Interior identifies the areas of the OCS it will offer for leasing and establishes a schedule for individual lease offerings. To develop a 5-year program under the OCS Lands Act, Interior is to consider several principles—including future national energy needs and location-specific factors, such as environmental sensitivity and marine productivity—and balance the potential for oil and gas discovery and adverse environmental effects. Interior also is to conduct leasing activities to ensure a fair market value to the federal government. In addition, Interior is to seek comments from various state and public stakeholders,

---

[12]In the western Gulf of Mexico, the technical term for a development plan is a Development and Operations Coordination Document.

[13]This process is usually considered to have four stages; however, for the purposes of this report, we are examining the process in six stages to separately discuss the issuance of drilling permits and inspections.

[14]Interior also permits geological and geophysical exploration outside the bounds of this process. These activities may introduce sounds into the ocean and have the potential to disrupt marine mammal behavior.

and prepare and release an EIS evaluating the likely effects of the 5-year program.

Stage 2: Planning and holding specific lease sales. After final approval of the nationwide 5-year program, Interior may hold lease sales under the OCS Lands Act for the lease parcels offered at auction. Laws protecting environmental resources—such as marine mammals, coastal birds, and wetlands—figure prominently at this stage. Under NEPA, before holding a lease sale, Interior is to evaluate the likely environmental effects of the proposed lease sale and describe various alternatives for oil and gas development and their potential environmental effects. In the Gulf of Mexico, Interior divides the region into three distinct planning areas—western, central, and eastern. For the western and central planning areas, Interior generally prepares a 5-year multilease sale EIS, which describes all lease sales scheduled for those planning areas of the Gulf of Mexico during that period and their potential environmental effects. Typically, Interior conducts one lease sale in the western and central planning areas each year. This EIS serves as the NEPA document for the first individual sales in those planning areas. Interior then typically conducts an EA or a supplemental EIS for the subsequent sales covered by the 5-year multilease sale EIS. For leases in the eastern planning area, most of which is currently under a leasing moratorium until 2022,[15] Interior generally prepares a separate EIS for any proposed activities that could affect resources in that area.

Because oil and gas development could affect species protected by the Endangered Species Act, Interior must also consult with the FWS and NOAA during this stage to assess the potential effects of oil and gas activities, including seismic exploration, on threatened and endangered species. Formal consultation between Interior and FWS and/or NOAA results in the issuance of a biological opinion on whether Interior's proposed actions are likely to jeopardize threatened or endangered species or adversely modify any designated critical habitat. As it relates to oil and gas development, the Endangered Species Act authorizes FWS and NOAA to allow incidental takings when approved through an

---

[15]A portion of the Central Gulf of Mexico Planning Area and most of the Eastern Gulf of Mexico Planning Area are under restriction until 2022 as part of the Gulf of Mexico Energy Security Act of 2006. The restricted areas include the portion of the eastern planning area within 125 miles of Florida, the Gulf of Mexico east of the Military Mission Line (86° 41' west longitude), and the central planning area located within 100 miles of Florida.

incidental take statement. The statement includes the amount or extent of anticipated take, reasonable and prudent measures to minimize the effects of incidental take, and the terms and conditions that must be observed.[16] Interior may use the "best available science" to assist in its determination during the consultation process. If Interior determines that the proposed federal action is not likely to adversely affect any endangered or threatened species, consultation may be concluded informally with concurrence from FWS and NOAA without preparation of a biological opinion. Oil and gas development could also affect species protected by the Marine Mammal Protection Act; therefore, Interior also coordinates with NOAA during this stage to mitigate potentially negative effects of oil and gas activities on marine mammals and obtain authorizations if mammals are likely to be taken. For offshore oil and gas development, oil and gas operators—or Interior, on behalf of operators—can apply to NOAA for an Incidental Take Authorization, which authorizes the incidental but not intentional taking of small numbers of marine mammals, provided the taking would have a negligible effect on marine mammals and no unmitigable adverse effect on subsistence use of marine mammals. Interior also is to consult with NOAA to ensure compliance with the Magnuson-Stevens Fishery Conservation and Management Act on actions that could adversely affect essential fish habitat, which is generally defined as areas necessary to fish for spawning, breeding, feeding, or growth to maturity. Additionally, Interior and NOAA completed a Programmatic Essential Fish Habitat Consultation in 1999, which is to be generally reviewed during development of Interior's Gulf of Mexico multilease sale EIS documents or when specific modifications are required.

During this stage, Interior is to coordinate with the five coastal Gulf of Mexico states through the Coastal Zone Management Act,[17] which helps states develop coastal management programs to manage and balance competing uses of the coastal zone. The act and implementing regulations require agency actions that are reasonably foreseeable to affect any land or water use, or natural resource of the coastal zone, to be consistent with enforceable policies of the five states' coastal management program. Accordingly, Interior is to provide the five states

---

[16]Take is defined under the Endangered Species Act as "to harass, harm, pursue, hunt, shoot, wound, kill, trap, capture, or collect, or to attempt to engage in any such conduct."

[17]The five coastal states are Alabama, Florida, Louisiana, Mississippi, and Texas.

with information for review during a designated period on lease sales and exploration and development plans to conduct a consistency determination—a review to determine if the proposed activities are consistent with the states' coastal management policies. If a coastal state determines that a proposed action by Interior is not consistent with the state's approved coastal zone management plan, it can pursue one of a number of administrative remedies.

At the end of this stage, Interior is to offer leases for competitive bidding, and all eligible companies are invited to submit written sealed bids for the rights to explore, develop, and produce oil and gas resources on these leases. The lease sale itself is a public auction, with leases sold to the highest qualified bidder. Interior may reject bids if it believes they are too low based on its analysis of the resource potential of a given lease.

Stage 3: Approving an operator's exploration plan. Before allowing an operator to explore for oil and gas in its leased area, Interior requires the operator to submit an exploration plan. The exploration plan is to describe all exploration activities planned by the operator, including the location of wells and timing of activities. The plan is to include an analysis of a "worst case" discharge from a potential spill and information on how the operator would respond to such a discharge.[18] After Interior receives an operator's exploration plan, it has 15 working days to review it for completeness. Once Interior determines a plan is deemed submitted, it has 30 calendar days to approve, disapprove, or require changes to the plan. When Interior requests changes or more information, the operator is to submit an amendment to the original plan, which begins new 15- and 30-day review periods. Interior is to review and approve the operator's exploration plan in accordance with the OCS Lands Act and prepare a NEPA analysis—typically tiered from the lease sale NEPA analysis completed in stage 2. In the Gulf of Mexico, Interior generally performs a NEPA categorical exclusion review to determine whether the planned activity can be excluded from further environmental analysis or if further environmental

---

[18]The worst case discharge analysis is the daily rate of an uncontrolled flow from all producible reservoirs into the open wellbore—the hole drilled from the seafloor down to the reservoir of oil or gas. The package of reservoirs exposed to an open wellbore with the greatest discharge potential is considered to be the worst case discharge scenario. Shallower producible reservoirs isolated by casing—a metal pipe that is inserted inside the wellbore to prevent high pressure fluids outside the formation from entering the well and to prevent drilling mud inside the well from fracturing fragile sections of the wellbore—and cement are not considered.

analysis is required. If, after conducting an initial environmental review, Interior determines that the planned activity does not involve "extraordinary circumstances"—which include potential effects to environmentally sensitive areas or resources, and public controversy over the environmental effects of the agency's proposed action—it may categorically exclude the plan from further environmental analysis.[19] However, if it determines that extraordinary circumstances are present, Interior is to prepare an EA or EIS, which may cause Interior to require modifications to the operator's exploration plan. Since August 2010, Interior has required EAs for deepwater exploration and development plans.[20] Interior is also to review each exploration plan to ensure that the plan is consistent with the affected states' coastal zone management plan.

Stage 4: Approving an operator's development and production plan. After the operator has determined that oil or gas can be found in the leased area and decides to begin development and production of a lease, the operator is to submit a development plan to Interior that describes the wells the operator plans to drill, where these wells will be located, the types of structures to be used, and how oil and natural gas will be transferred to shore. Interior has 25 working days to deem the plan submitted or notify the operator of problems that prevent it from being deemed submitted. Once Interior determines the plan is deemed submitted, it has 120 calendar days to approve, disapprove, or require changes to the plan. When Interior requests changes or more information, the operator is to submit an amendment to the original plan, which begins a new 25-working day and 120-calendar day review period. Under the OCS Lands Act, Interior is to review each development and production plan to assess potential environmental effects and ensure that the plan is consistent with the affected states' coastal zone management plan. Similar to Interior's review of exploration plans in the Gulf of Mexico region, Interior is to prepare a NEPA categorical exclusion review to determine whether the planned activity may be categorically excluded from further NEPA review. Since August 2010, Interior has required EAs

---

[19]Under NEPA, if an agency determines that activities of a proposed project fall within a category of activities the agency has already determined have no significant environmental effect—called a categorical exclusion—then the agency generally does not need to prepare an EA or an EIS.

[20]Interior specifically requires preparation of an EA for exploration plans involving subsea blowout preventers or drilling from floating facilities, which are generally associated with deepwater operations.

for deepwater exploration and development plans. On the basis of this final NEPA analysis, operators are to secure Interior's approval of their development plans before proceeding past the exploration stage.

Stage 5: Approving an operator's drilling permit. Once Interior approves an operator's plan, the operator is required to obtain drilling permits from Interior for wells specified in either the exploration or development plan. The operator submits an application for a drilling permit to the appropriate Interior district office, where a district engineer initially is to review it for completeness and compliance with regulation. The drilling permit may be for a new well, which is the first time an operator drills a wellbore—the hole drilled from the seafloor down to the reservoir of oil or gas—at a location; a bypass, which is when an operator drills around an obstruction in the current wellbore; or a sidetrack, which is when an operator uses the current wellbore to drill into a new oil or gas reservoir.[21] The operator's application may also include a request for a departure—or a waiver from complying with a particular regulation. Interior's district engineer is to review the technical elements of the application and verify that they conform to all applicable federal regulations.[22] This review includes verifying that the blowout preventer—a piece of equipment designed to prevent the uncontrolled flow of oil and gas from a well—is appropriate for the well design. Additionally, the engineer is to review plans for the well's technical specifications, including the casing and cementing specifications, among other items. At this point, the district engineer may approve the permit. In some instances, however, the district engineer may return the permit to the operator for incompleteness or correction and resubmission. Unlike exploration and development plans, Interior has no statutory time frames for making a final decision on a drilling permit. Only after Interior approves a permit can drilling begin.[23] Once drilling is

---

[21]Each of these types of drilling permits can be revised, and each revision also requires an application and Interior approval.

[22]In addition to regulations developed by Interior, Interior incorporates standards into its regulations that have been generally agreed upon by industry and regulators and published by the American Petroleum Institute (API). Since the passage of the National Technology Transfer and Advancement Act in 1996, federal agencies have been required to adopt private-sector standards, such as API's, wherever practical, in lieu of creating their own proprietary, nonconsensus standards.

[23]During drilling operations, operators submit a well activity report to district engineers on a weekly basis that includes a description of the drilling activities. The operator can also report whether one of twelve significant events occurred, such as drilling rig equipment failures.

completed, if the operator determines that oil and gas can be economically produced from the well, the operator submits an application to the appropriate Interior regional office to begin production.

Stage 6: Inspecting offshore oil and gas activities. Interior inspectors from the five district offices are to conduct inspections in the Gulf of Mexico to ensure that operators are in compliance with all regulatory requirements.[24] Weather permitting, inspectors fly via helicopter to an offshore drilling rig or production platform to conduct inspections and generally return at the end of the day. The primary objective of an initial inspection is to ensure proper installation and functionality of operational components along with the associated safety and pollution prevention equipment on drilling rigs and production platforms. After drilling operations begin, Interior conducts additional inspections. Under the OCS Lands Act, Interior is required to inspect offshore facilities, including production platforms and drilling rigs, on an annual basis, but Interior officials told us that they have an informal goal of conducting inspections on drilling rigs once per month. The act also authorizes Interior to provide for both annual scheduled—or announced—inspections and periodic unscheduled—or unannounced—inspections of all OCS oil and gas operations, including those in the Gulf of Mexico. During inspections, Interior inspectors are to adhere to specific guidelines established by regulation and Interior-approved plans and permits. The inspectors perform the inspections, in part through using a checklist called the Potential Incident of Noncompliance list, which is a compilation of yes or no questions derived from regulated safety and environmental requirements. If an inspector identifies out of compliance activities at an offshore facility, a nonfinancial violation is issued, which may be (1) a warning, (2) an order to shut down a particular component of the facility, or (3) an order to shut down an entire drilling rig or production platform. Operators generally have 14 days to correct the violation and notify Interior that the violation was corrected. Interior's policy is to place

---

[24]In 2004, Interior and the Coast Guard signed a memorandum of understanding (MOU) to delineate inspection responsibilities between the agencies. Under the MOU, Interior is responsible for, among other things, managing the nation's oil, natural gas, and other mineral resources on the OCS in a safe and environmentally sound manner. The MOU assigns the Coast Guard the responsibility for ensuring (1) the safety of life and property on offshore energy facilities and vessels engaged in OCS activities; (2) workplace safety and health, including enforcement of requirements related to personnel, workplace activities, and conditions and equipment on the OCS; and (3) security of offshore energy facilities.

operators with a history of poor performance on its monthly operator compliance list and inspect those operators more frequently until it determines that the operator's performance has improved.

Interior also administers a civil penalties program with the goal of ensuring safe and environmentally sound operations on the OCS.[25] If an inspector identifies a violation such as one that could cause injury, death, environmental damage, or threaten human life or the environment, Interior is to review the violation for a civil penalty assessment review. However, before a civil penalty case is officially opened, both the district's supervisory inspector and district manager are to review the violation. A civil penalty case is officially opened only after the district manager agrees with the inspector and forwards the violation to an Interior civil penalty reviewing officer in the relevant regional office. Once a case is opened, the civil penalty reviewing officer may develop the case by collecting additional information about the violation. If the reviewing officer determines that a violation met Interior's criteria—which includes whether the violation caused injury, death, or environmental damage or posed a threat to human life or the environment—Interior may issue the operator a financial penalty. However, the reviewing officer may also determine that a civil penalty is not warranted, in which case Interior would close the civil penalty case. In addition to assessing a financial penalty, Interior may also suspend any operation on the OCS, including in the Gulf of Mexico region, if an operator fails to comply with a provision of any applicable law, regulation, or order or provision of a lease or permit.[26]

Recent Policy Changes Intended to Improve Offshore Oil and Gas Activities

Interior has enacted numerous policy changes intended to improve Interior's oversight of offshore oil and gas activities on the OCS, including in the Gulf of Mexico since the *Deepwater Horizon* incident. As part of its oversight responsibilities, Interior issues guidance documents called Notices to Lessees and Operators that clarify, supplement, or provide more detail about certain requirements. In response to the *Deepwater Horizon* incident, Interior issued three of these notices, which, among other things, notified operators that Interior would be evaluating whether they had submitted adequate well containment information with their oil

---

[25]30 C.F.R. Part 250, Subpart N.

[26]30 C.F.R. § 250.173(a).

spill response plans.[27] Specifically, in one notice, Interior informed operators that it would evaluate whether they could demonstrate that they had access to and could deploy well containment resources to adequately and promptly respond to a blowout—the uncontrolled release of oil or gas from a well on the ocean floor or other loss of well control (see fig. 4).

---

[27]Containment refers to measures taken—after a major oil spill event such as a blowout—to prevent more oil and gas from reaching the environment. Oil spill response plans must include an operator's proposed methods for ensuring that oil spill containment and recovery equipment and response personnel are mobilized and deployed in the event of a spill.

Figure 4: Timeline of Key Events Since the *Deepwater Horizon* Incident

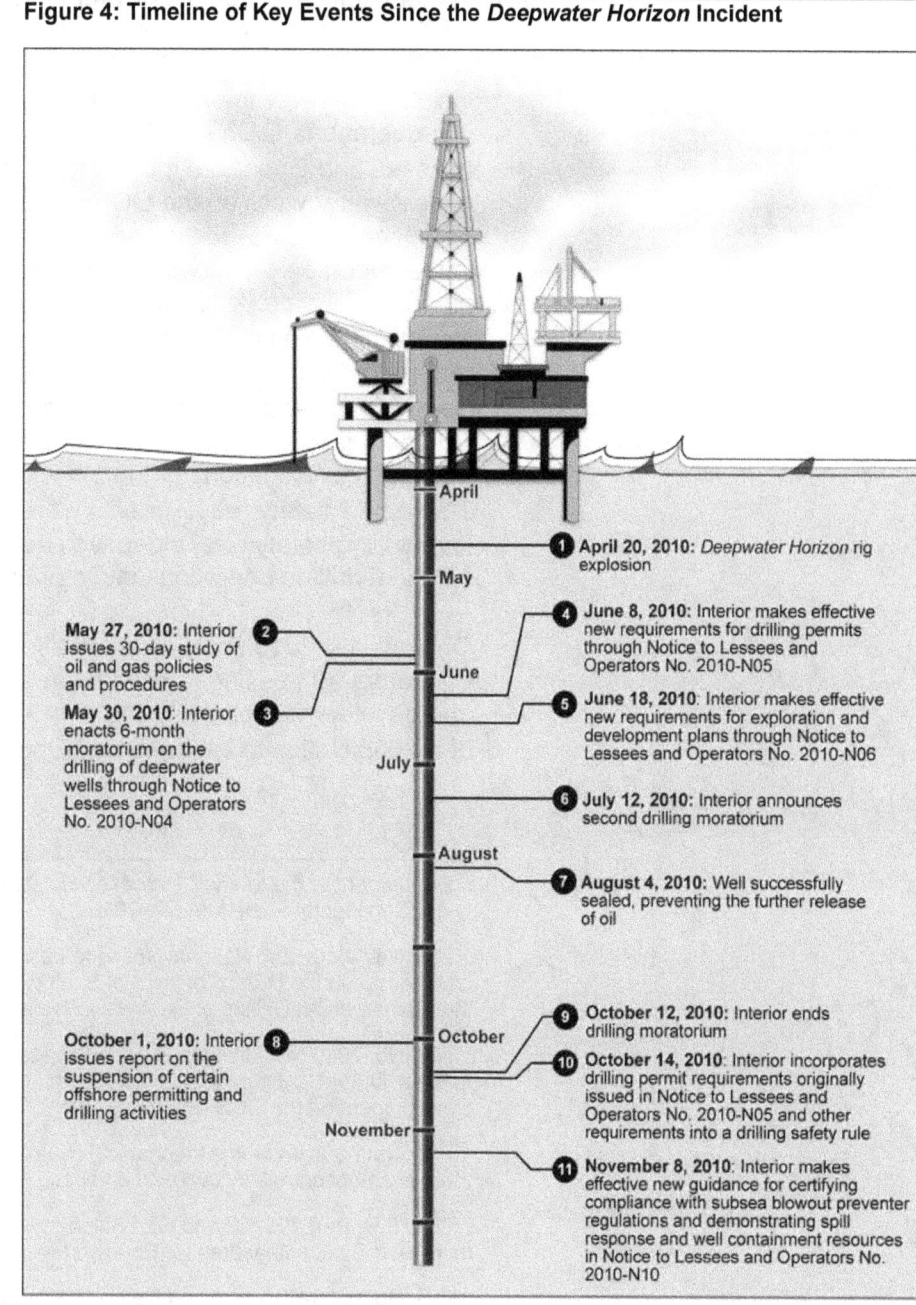

Source: GAO and MapArt.

Immediately after the *Deepwater Horizon* incident, the President ordered the Secretary of the Interior to complete a 30-day study of its offshore oil and gas policies and procedures, resulting in a May 27, 2010, report that included 22 recommendations for improving the safety of offshore oil and gas operations.[28] On May 30, 2010, Interior made effective a Notice to Lessees and Operators that enacted a 6-month moratorium on the drilling of deepwater wells on the OCS, including the Gulf of Mexico, in light of significant risks associated with drilling in deepwater without implementation of recommendations from the report on safety equipment, practices, and procedures.[29] On June 8, 2010, Interior made effective a Notice to Lessees and Operators that included seven new safety requirements for drilling permits as recommended in the report.[30] These new requirements include certification by an operator's Chief Executive Officer that operations were in compliance with Interior's regulations, and third party certifications of the blowout preventer,[31] among other items. These new safety requirements were later incorporated into an interim final drilling safety rule, along with additional requirements to enhance the safety of drilling operations in October 2010.[32]

On June 18, 2010, Interior made effective a Notice to Lessees and Operators addressing revised information requirements for exploration and development plans.[33] The policy, among other things, reversed part of a 2008 Notice to Lessees and Operators that limited the information

---

[28]Department of the Interior. Increased Safety Measures for Energy Development on the Outer Continental Shelf. May 27, 2010.

[29]NTL No. 2010-N04. National Notice to Lessees and Operators (NTL) of Federal Oil and Gas Leases in the Outer Continental Shelf (OCS): To Implement the Directive to Impose a Moratorium on All Drilling of Deepwater Wells. Effective May 30, 2010.

[30]NTL No. 2010-N05. National Notice to Lessees and Operators of Federal Oil and Gas Leases, Outer Continental Shelf (OCS): Increased Safety measures for Energy Development on the OCS. Effective June 8, 2010.

[31]A blowout preventer is a mechanical device intended to control and close off a well if there is an uncontrolled flow of oil and gas.

[32]30 C.F.R. Part 250. Oil and Gas Sulphur Operations in the Outer Continental Shelf-Increased Safety Measures for Energy Development on the Outer Continental Shelf.

[33]NTL No. 2010-N06. National Notice to Lessees and Operators of Federal Oil and Gas Leases, Outer Continental Shelf (OCS): Information Requirements for Exploration Plans, Development and Production Plans, and Development Operations Coordination Documents on the OCS. Effective June 18, 2010.

operators were required to submit regarding blowout scenarios and worst-case discharge scenarios.[34,35] The new policy required that operators submit more detailed information about their worst case discharge scenarios and blowout scenarios in exploration, development, and oil spill response plans. The new policy explained that all operators, regardless of location or state coordination, must submit more detailed information. Along with the June 18, 2010, Notice to Lessees and Operators, Interior released, and updated three times, a list of frequently asked questions as a means to provide operators with additional guidance on how to comply with the new policies.[36]

In June 2010, several companies filed a lawsuit related to the deepwater drilling moratorium against the Secretary of the Interior. On June 22, 2010, a U.S. District Court overturned Interior's initial drilling suspension.[37] Interior then announced a second drilling moratorium on July 12, 2010, noting the following three key factors as the basis for the decision: (1) it provided Interior, industry, and others time to develop strategies and methods for the containment of uncontrolled wells in deepwater; (2) it was necessary to ensure that an appropriate and sufficient response was available in the event of another major oil spill; and (3) it allowed for the collection and analysis of evidence regarding the potential causes of the *Deepwater Horizon* incident. On August 16, 2010, Interior issued a memorandum which directed all deepwater drilling plans to be analyzed with EAs instead of relying on categorical exclusion reviews. On October 1, 2010, Interior issued a report on the suspension of certain offshore permitting and drilling activities.[38] Additionally, many of the revised policies outlined in the notices were incorporated into new

---

[34]A blowout scenario includes information on the estimated oil and gas flow rate, total volume, and maximum duration of a blowout.

[35]NTL No. 2008-G04. Notice to Lessees and Operators of Federal Oil, Gas, and Sulphur Leases in the Outer Continental Shelf, Gulf of Mexico OCS Region: Information Requirements for Exploration Plans and Development Operations Coordination Documents. Effective May 1, 2008. Expiration March 31, 2013.

[36]NTL No. 2010-N06. Frequently Asked Questions. Effective June 18, 2010 with updates on July 15, July 21, and August 10, 2010.

[37]Honbeck Offshore Servs., L.L.C. v. Salazar, 696 F. Supp. 2d. 627 (E.D. La. 2010).

[38]Department of the Interior. Decision Memorandum. Report Regarding the Current Suspension of Certain Offshore Permitting and Drilling Activities on the Outer Continental Shelf. Issued on October 1, 2010.

GAO-12-423 Oil and Gas Management

regulations via Interior's emergency rule process. The Secretary of the Interior ended the drilling moratorium on October 12, 2010, but directed that, before any drilling permits were issued, operators had to certify compliance with all existing rules and requirements, including those recently implemented, and demonstrate the availability of adequate blowout containment resources. On October 14, 2010, Interior published an interim final drilling safety rule that incorporated new safety requirements, some of which were previously issued in a Notice to Lessees and Operators, along with additional requirements to enhance the safety of drilling operations.[39] On November 8, 2010, Interior made effective another Notice to Lessees and Operators requiring operators conducting activities using subsea blowout preventers or surface blowout preventers on floating facilities to provide Interior with adequate information demonstrating that they have access to and can deploy containment resources to promptly respond to a blowout or other loss of well control.[40] On December 13, 2010, Interior released a document to provide operators further guidance regarding environmental and safety requirements to be used in preparing their plans and permits.

Interior Has Generally Met Its Key Reorganization Time Frames

On October 1, 2011, Interior generally met its key reorganization time frame by officially reorganizing its oversight of offshore oil and gas activities in the Gulf of Mexico with the establishment of two new bureaus. To aid the development of these new bureaus, the Secretary of the Interior directed Interior staff to develop an implementation plan to provide further details on the planned reorganization, including target dates. Because the oversight responsibilities of these two new bureaus have many interdependencies, and their success will depend on effective coordination, Interior has drafted memorandums and standard operating procedures to define their roles and responsibilities and facilitate and formalize their coordination.

---

[39]Oil and Gas and Sulfur Operations in the Outer Continental Shelf—Increased Safety Measures for Energy Development on the Outer Continental Shelf, 75 *Fed. Reg.* 63346 (2010).

[40]NTL No. 2010-N10. National Notice to Lessees and Operators (NTL) of Federal Oil and Gas Leases, Outer Continental Shelf: Statement of Compliance with Applicable Regulations and Evaluation of Information Demonstrating Adequate Spill Response and Well Containment. Effective November 8, 2010.

Interior Established Two Independent Bureaus, Separating Resource Management from Safety and Environmental Oversight and Enforcement

On October 1, 2011, Interior met its goal to establish two new independent bureaus to oversee offshore oil and gas activities on the OCS, including in the Gulf of Mexico, effectively separating Interior's mission to manage resources from its mission to provide oversight of safety and environmental enforcement. On May 19, 2010, following the *Deepwater Horizon* incident, the Secretary of the Interior signed a secretarial order to reorganize the roles and responsibilities performed by MMS into new management structures. Interior subsequently contracted with a consultant and formed an agency taskforce to develop key milestones for the reorganization.[41] According to the secretarial order, the goals of the reorganization were to improve the management, oversight, and accountability of activities on the OCS; ensure a fair return to the taxpayer from royalty and revenue collection and disbursement activities; and provide independent safety and environmental oversight and enforcement of offshore activities. In the reorganization, Interior renamed MMS to BOEMRE as an interim step before transferring MMS's oil and gas revenue collection functions to the newly created Office of Natural Resources Revenue and separating BOEMRE into two bureaus—BOEM and BSEE.[42] To divide BOEMRE's responsibilities, Interior issued new regulations in October 2011 reorganizing existing regulations under the new bureaus, thereby formally separating Interior's regulations that govern leasing and approval of development from those addressing lease operations, safety, and enforcement.[43] Specifically, under the reorganization, BOEM is to oversee resource management activities, including preparing the 5-year OCS oil and gas leasing program; reviewing oil and gas exploration and development plans and environmental studies; and conducting NEPA analyses. BSEE is to oversee operations and environmental compliance, including reviewing drilling permits, inspecting offshore drilling rigs and production platforms, assessing civil penalties, and developing regulations and standards for offshore drilling. Additionally, BSEE is to manage the National Offshore

---

[41]Department of the Interior, *Establishment of the Bureau of Ocean Energy Management, the Bureau of Safety and Environmental Enforcement, and the Office of Natural Resources Revenue*, Order No. 3299 (May 19, 2010).

[42]Department of Interior, *Change of the Name of the Minerals Management Service to the Bureau of Ocean Energy Management, Regulation, and Enforcement*, Order No. 3302 (June 18, 2010).

[43]Reorganization of Title 30: Bureaus of Safety and Environmental Enforcement and Ocean Energy Management (Direct final rule). 76 *Fed. Reg.* 64432 (2011).

Training and Learning Center—established in June 2011—to train its inspectors and engineers. (See fig. 5 for a high level illustration of the reorganization and app. II for the full organizational charts for both BOEM and BSEE.)

Figure 5: Interior's Key Offshore Oil and Gas Program Responsibilities before and after Reorganization

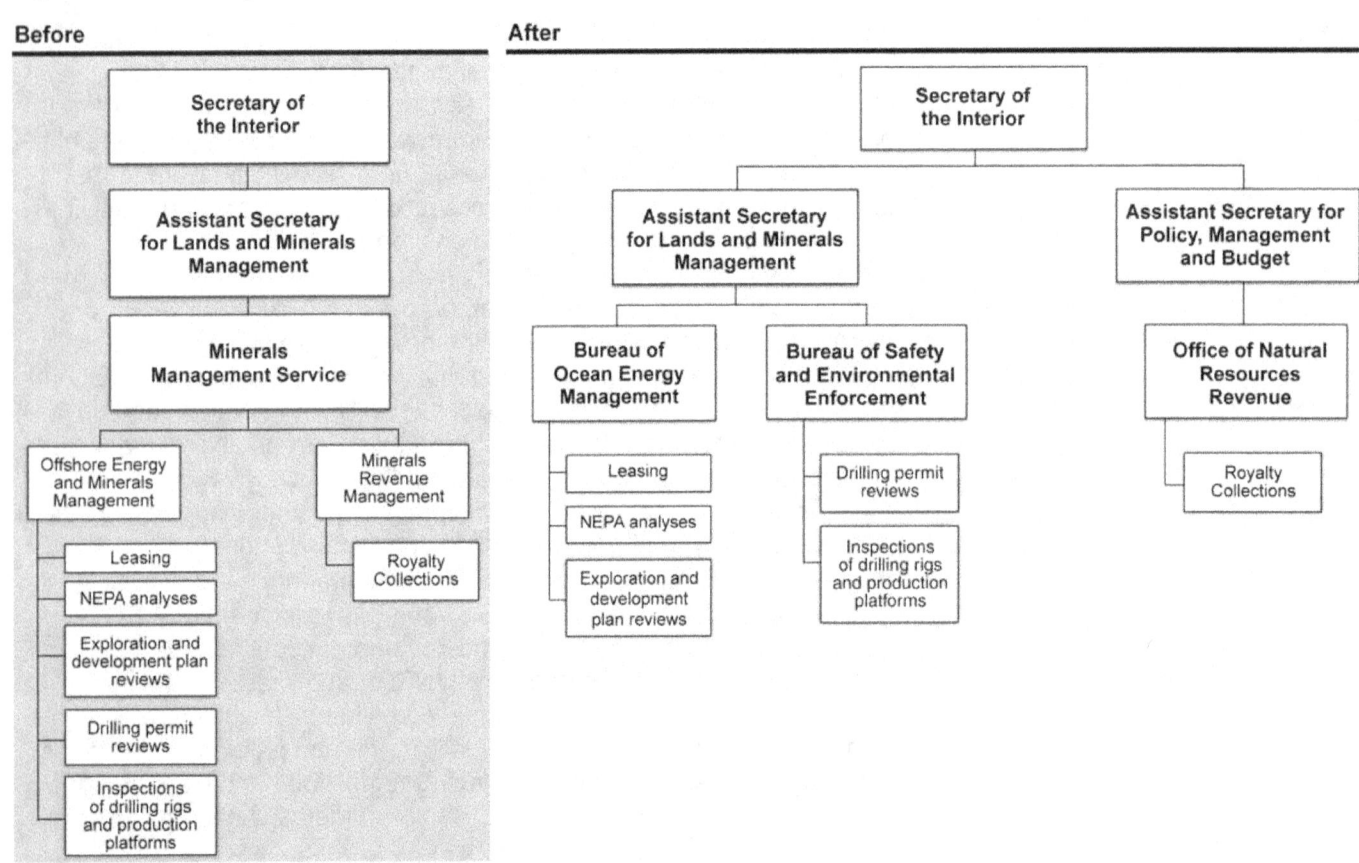

Source: GAO.

Interior and others identified a number of reasons for dividing the roles and responsibilities previously performed by MMS. BOEMRE's director noted that MMS had three competing missions—revenue collection, energy development, and safety and environmental enforcement. The National Commission on the BP *Deepwater Horizon* Oil Spill and Offshore Drilling concluded that MMS had primarily focused on revenue collection and energy development, adversely affecting its ability to set and enforce appropriate safety and environmental oversight rules. After the

Deepwater Horizon incident, the President directed Interior to provide a postaccident safety report within 30 days. While developing this report, Interior's senior management, including the Secretary, discussed dividing MMS's duties. A senior Interior official stated that, even before the *Deepwater Horizon* incident, Interior's leadership was considering alternative management structures to MMS, noting that separating resource management from the safety and environmental enforcement functions had been a best practice used by some European nations such as Norway, which established the Petroleum Safety Authority in January 2004 to hold regulatory responsibility for safety, emergency preparedness, and the working environment in the petroleum activities. Previously, these responsibilities were held under the Norwegian Petroleum Directorate, which among other responsibilities oversees resource management.

Some Interior officials stated that they expect Interior's overall management of oil and gas resources to improve due to the reorganization. A senior Interior official overseeing the reorganization stated that establishing three separate bureaus, each with its own director, will help ensure equal advocacy for all three missions. For example, the official stated that by establishing BSEE, the director of BSEE will be responsible for safety and environmental enforcement, independent from the resource management development and revenue collection missions. In addition, an official in the Gulf of Mexico regional office stated that by reducing the scope of each bureau's mission,[44] the responsibilities of the regional managers will also be reduced so that they may delegate less, focus more on the areas they oversee, and take a more hands-on approach to management.

Interior's Implementation Plan Guided the Reorganization

To aid the establishment of the new bureaus, the secretarial order directed that an implementation plan with a schedule for the planned reorganization be developed within 30 days.[45] In July 2010, Interior issued its implementation plan with target dates, including October 1, 2011, as the target date to complete the reorganization. The

---

[44]Because many of our interviews were conducted with Interior officials before BSEE and BOEM were established, we generally do not distinguish the bureau of the official but refer to them as Interior officials.

[45]Sec. Order No. 3299.

implementation plan also provided target dates for completing tasks to facilitate the reorganization, including reports of best practices and organizational effectiveness and a detailed organizational structure for BOEM and BSEE. A senior Interior official stated that, although the implementation plan identified target dates for the reorganization, details of the reorganization were not developed until later in the process.

According to a senior Interior official, the primary decisions about the reorganization were made by BOEMRE's director, with input from senior advisors, including both political appointees and career Interior management staff. To help inform these decisions and complete tasks, Interior hired a consultant at a cost of approximately $7 million, as of November 2011,[46] and created an agency taskforce—a team of over 65 Interior staff with multiple subteams focused on identifying interdependencies between BOEM and BSEE.[47] Interior officials stated that the expertise and advice provided by the consultant was critical to completing the reorganization on time while simultaneously keeping the agency's regulatory processes operating, and positioning both new bureaus to operate effectively at start up. Throughout this process, according to a senior Interior official, the consultant worked closely with the taskforce. The consultant was responsible for developing a series of reports specified in the July 2010 implementation plan and contract as well as providing guidance to BOEMRE management on how to conduct analyses that supported key reorganizational decisions. According to a senior Interior official, the consultant provided reports from September 2010 through February of 2011 that helped inform the reorganization. These reports included assessments of (1) BOEMRE's organizational structure based, in part, on over 200 interviews, according to the consultant, (2) relevant regulatory best practices from Canada's and Norway's offshore oil and gas regulators, as well as the U.S. Department of Agriculture's and Nuclear Regulatory Commission's inspection

---

[46]The contract included a base period as well as several options that were exercised by Interior to provide consulting services throughout the reorganization process. In addition to the approximately $7 million identified earlier, the contract includes an additional option to purchase approximately $1 million in consulting services.

[47]This taskforce is consistent with our July 2003 report in which we discuss key practices and implementation steps for successful organizational transformations, including the use of dedicated implementation teams as well as the involvement of employees to obtain their ideas and gain ownership for the transformation.GAO, *Results Oriented Cultures: Implementation Steps to Assist Mergers and Organizational Transformations*, GAO-03-669 (Washington, D.C.: July 2, 2003).

programs, (3) organizational options for dividing BOEMRE's responsibilities into BOEM and BSEE, and (4) an implementation plan detailing the necessary steps to complete the reorganization within specified time frames, among other assessments. Following the issuance of the consultant's February 2011 report, the consultant continued to assist the reorganization.

The taskforce's primary goal was to help ensure that BOEM and BSEE were fully functional as of October 1, 2011, in accordance with the target date outlined in the implementation plan. Among other activities, the taskforce helped determine BOEM's and BSEE's future organizational structures, identified interdependencies between BOEM and BSEE, and developed standard operating procedures to help manage functions across the two bureaus. Specifically, while working with the consultant, the taskforce identified 49 interdependencies between BOEM and BSEE, such as between BOEM's leasing responsibilities and BSEE's district office engineers' responsibilities. Of those 49 interdependencies, the taskforce identified 16 that required policy solutions, including, for example, ensuring that drilling permit information is available to BSEE's district engineers, as well as BOEM staff responsible for reviewing and approving exploration and development plans. The taskforce developed potential policy solutions for many of these interdependencies and provided them to Interior senior managers, including BOEMRE's director.

Interior took other steps to support the separation of BOEMRE into BOEM and BSEE, including dividing the two bureaus' financial records, although BSEE manages administrative resources—such as IT resources—for both bureaus to achieve cost savings. Interior also officially reassigned employees and launched separate websites for each bureau.

Interior Has Developed an MOU for BOEM and BSEE to Facilitate Coordination

According to Interior officials, BOEM and BSEE will maintain a close working relationship, particularly during the early stages of their formation, due to the interdependencies in their oversight responsibilities. Prior to the division of BOEMRE, a senior Interior official in the Gulf of Mexico Regional office stated that the split would not "put up a wall" between the two bureaus, noting that both bureaus will continue to occupy the same New Orleans, Louisiana, building and that staff would be able to "walk down the hall" to discuss and resolve issues with colleagues in both bureaus. Interior officials further stated that the initial reorganization will not significantly change the bureau's work processes.

To help define BOEM's and BSEE's roles and responsibilities and facilitate and formalize their collaboration, Interior developed an overarching inter-bureau MOU; a six program set of area-specific memoranda of agreements; and numerous standard operating procedures. The MOU establishes a high-level working relationship between BOEM and BSEE and, according to the document, is intended to help minimize duplication of effort, promote consistency in procedures and regulations, and resolve disputes between the two bureaus. To help accomplish these goals, the MOU outlines a number of postreorganization roles and responsibilities. For example, it calls for the deputy directors of BOEM and BSEE to meet at least quarterly to discuss means to better ensure collaboration across the bureaus. The MOU also outlines the use of the six memoranda of agreements to establish principles for collaboration on program areas across BOEM and BSEE including: (1) plans and permits; (2) the environment and NEPA; (3) geologic data assignments; (4) the marine minerals program; (5) assignments, bonding, and pipelines; and (6) royalty relief requests. Each memorandum of agreement outlines roles and responsibilities for BOEM and BSEE and references a number of standard operating procedures that document interdependencies between the bureaus. Each standard operating procedure identifies specific objectives, responsibilities, and agency interdependencies for specific work actions. In documenting agency interdependencies, each standard operating procedure provides details on the actions to be taken by BSEE and BOEM for individual program activities. An Interior official said that, over time, the standard operating procedures will be refined and that it will be important to clearly document changes to them in order to minimize the risk of staff relying on institutional knowledge, especially as experienced staff retire or find work elsewhere.

Key Policy Changes for Oil and Gas NEPA Analyses, Plans, and Permits Intended to Enhance Oversight Initially Increased Review Times and Resource Requirements

Key policy changes Interior has implemented since the *Deepwater Horizon* incident, which were designed to mitigate the risk of a well blowout or spill, initially required Interior to devote additional resources and time to reviewing oil and gas exploration and development plans and drilling permits for oil and gas activities on the OCS, including in the Gulf of Mexico. Specifically, these policy changes affected Interior's (1) NEPA analyses for oil and gas exploration and development plans, including its use of categorical exclusions; (2) reviews of oil and gas exploration and development plans; and (3) reviews of oil and gas drilling permits.

Interior Relied Heavily on Categorical Exclusions, but Use Is Now Limited Pending an Internal Review

Interior approved almost all exploration plans (97 percent) and development plans (98 percent) for oil and gas activities in the Gulf of Mexico from January 1, 2000, through April 19, 2010, using a categorical exclusion. That is, because Interior had previously determined that a planned activity was not likely to significantly affect the environment, it categorically excluded the activity from a more detailed, site-specific NEPA analysis.

Of the 3,249 exploration plans Interior approved from January 1, 2000, through April 19, 2010, approximately 14 percent were approved via a categorical exclusion with no additional analysis; 83 percent were approved via categorical exclusion with some additional analysis; and 3 percent were approved via a more detailed, site-specific EA.[48] Interior officials told us they prepared EA documents for exploration plans for several reasons, including plans for (1) development in the eastern Gulf of Mexico, (2) using new and unusual technology, or (3) development adjacent to the federally protected Flower Garden Banks National Marine Sanctuary. The overall results for development plans were similar. Of the 2,935 approved development plans submitted, approximately 16 percent were approved via a categorical exclusion with no additional analysis, 82 percent were approved via a categorical exclusion with some additional

---

[48]Approximately 2 percent of approved exploration plans were missing a NEPA code and were not included in our analysis.

analysis, and 2 percent were approved via a more detailed, site-specific EA[49] (see fig. 6).

Figure 6: Interior's NEPA Determination for Approved Plans from January 1, 2000, through April 19, 2010

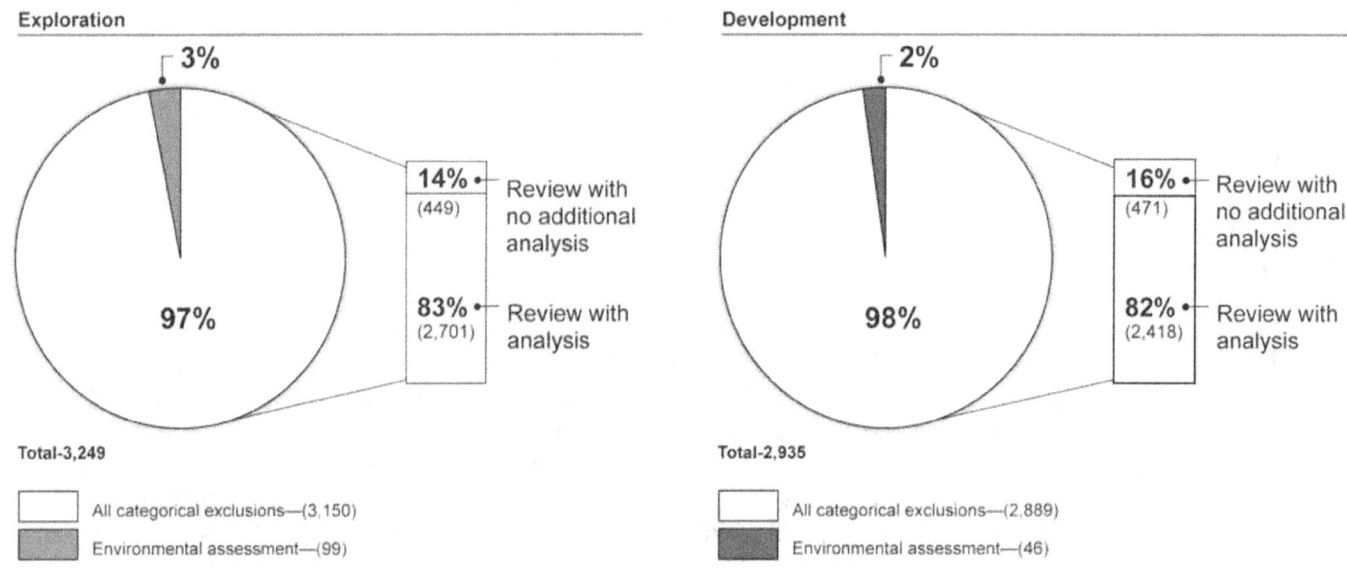

Source: GAO analysis of Interior data.

Categorical Exclusion Reviews Were Hindered by Poor Geographic Information System Data Quality, a Lack of Controls, and Limited Criteria

Interior's categorical exclusion reviews were hindered by (1) the poor quality of data in Interior's geographic information system (GIS), (2) limited controls for ensuring NEPA analyses for approved plans were based on complete and accurate information, and (3) limited clear criteria for identifying certain types of activities that may preclude the use of categorical exclusions. According to Interior's policy prior to the *Deepwater Horizon* incident, all exploration and development plans underwent a NEPA analysis, called a categorical exclusion review to determine whether the operator proposed activities could be categorically excluded from further analysis or if the plan required an EA or EIS. The categorical exclusion review—though less detailed and thorough than an EA or EIS—consisted of a series of environmental evaluations and site-specific, environmental resource reviews. These site-specific reviews, which are based largely on

---

[49]Approximately 2 percent of approved development plans were missing a NEPA code and were not included in our analysis.

information in Interior's GIS, include assessments of the effects of oil and gas activities on air and water quality, archeological sites, and biologically sensitive areas, among others.

However, according to Interior officials, Interior has been unable to maintain complete and accurate data in its GIS system due to limited resources. Interior officials stated that they have developed alternative processes to compensate for the current GIS limitations; however, these processes are time and resource intensive and prone to error. Because Interior relies on GIS data to conduct its categorical exclusion reviews to determine whether additional environmental analyses are necessary, and these data may be incomplete and inaccurate, by using them there is a risk of not accurately assessing a plan's potential environmental effects or identifying plans that might warrant a more detailed environmental analysis. Interior officials told us that they have begun to devote resources to improving Interior's GIS data and that the GIS is being upgraded and is scheduled to be deployed in May 2012.

We also found that Interior's current plan review process could cause it to approve a plan where the NEPA analysis, including categorical exclusion reviews, was based on incomplete or inaccurate information. According to Interior's policy, exploration and development plans undergo a NEPA analysis through a categorical exclusion review in order to determine whether the activity can be categorically excluded or if the plan requires additional review through an EA or EIS.[50] Interior's NEPA staff conduct these reviews. However, during the exploration and development plan review process, Interior officials explained that they may request that operators provide additional information or correct previously submitted information through a plan amendment. Sometimes, according to Interior officials, these amendments may contain information necessary for completing the NEPA analysis. In such cases, Interior officials told us that staff reviewing the plan are to coordinate with NEPA staff to ensure that any information included in subsequent amendments would not need to be considered as part of a NEPA analysis. However, Interior staff stated that this coordination does not always occur and that this coordination is not documented in Interior's Technical Information Management System (TIMS) IT system, meaning that Interior cannot be confident that its NEPA

---

[50]Since the *Deepwater Horizon* incident, Interior no longer used the categorical exclusion review process for deepwater exploration and development plans.

analyses were based on the most current relevant information in the exploration and development plans. For example, in one instance, the NEPA analysis was completed before Interior had received an operator's plan amendment, which included the operator's final worst case scenario discharge estimate, information that, according to Interior officials, would typically be considered during Interior's NEPA analysis. Interior officials acknowledged that the controls in place are insufficient to prevent the approval of plans with NEPA analyses that were based on inaccurate or incomplete information. Without complete and accurate information to analyze the potential effects of a proposed project as required by NEPA, Interior risks making an erroneous assessment of the environmental risks associated with such a project.

Our analysis of Interior's data on approved exploration and development plans that had amendments from January 1, 2000, through April 19, 2010, found that, for about 15 percent of the 1,466 plans it approved, Interior completed its NEPA analysis, including categorical exclusion reviews, before all of the plan's final amendments had been submitted (see fig. 7).

Figure 7: Approved Plans Amended after Final NEPA Determination Was Made, January 1, 2000, through April 19, 2010

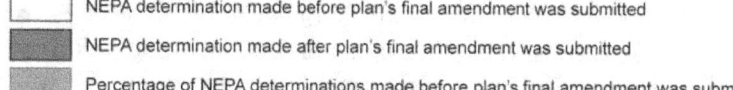

Number of plans

NEPA determination made before plan's final amendment was submitted

NEPA determination made after plan's final amendment was submitted

Percentage of NEPA determinations made before plan's final amendment was submitted

Source: GAO analysis of Interior data.

In addition, we found that Interior does not have clear criteria for certain types of activities that preclude the use of categorical exclusions. Interior policy states that if a categorical exclusion review concludes that a proposed activity could result in an "extraordinary circumstance," such as having highly uncertain or potentially significant environmental effects, Interior cannot approve the plan through a categorical exclusion and must prepare, at a minimum, an EA.[51] Extraordinary circumstances include

---

[51]Interior policy allowed approval of exploratory and development plans in the Western and Central Gulf of Mexico—since 1981 and 1985, respectively—via categorical exclusions, except when staff determined that an extraordinary circumstance existed. The initial policy of categorically excluding exploration and development plans in the Western Gulf of Mexico, according to Interior officials, was carried over from the U.S. Geological Survey, which had regulatory authority over the Gulf of Mexico prior to the creation of MMS in 1982. Interior officials reported that the policy for approving plans via categorical exclusions was based on the findings of numerous previously completed EA documents that resulted in a finding of no significant effect.

actions such as approving a development plan (1) in areas of high seismic risk or seismicity, relatively untested waters, or remote areas; (2) within the boundary of a proposed or established marine sanctuary, or within or near the boundary of a proposed or established wildlife refuge or areas of high biological sensitivity; (3) in areas of hazardous natural bottom conditions; or (4) utilizing new or unusual technology. Additionally, Interior's departmental manual specifies a number of "exceptions" to individual actions within categorical exclusions—such as activities with highly controversial or very uncertain environmental effects or activities that could potentially adversely affect endangered species—and requires that Interior prepare an EA or EIS for such actions. Interior officials told us that, while certain extraordinary circumstances and exceptions, such as those related to endangered species, are more clearly determined and would trigger an EA or EIS, others have less precise criteria, and according to Interior policy, the responsible official determines whether they are significant. For example, Interior officials told us that Interior does not have documented clear criteria on what constitutes a controversial environmental effect as it relates to an exploration or development plan; instead, Interior has relied on the expertise of its staff to identify such cases. Additionally, these officials stated that Interior does not have clear criteria on what constitutes new or unusual technology. Interior officials told us that there was an effort to develop guidance on this issue, but that such guidance was never completed. Without documented clear criteria for when staff may categorically exclude a plan from a more detailed, NEPA analysis, Interior risks making inconsistent determinations as to what constitutes an extraordinary circumstance and making insufficient assessments of the potential effects of a proposed plan. According to Interior officials, Interior issued a NEPA handbook in September 2011 in response to a recommendation from our March 2010 report, in which we recommended that Interior develop and set a deadline for issuing a comprehensive NEPA handbook providing guidance on how to implement NEPA and periodically update and revise this guidance as needed.[52] Interior officials stated that, while additional guidance on extraordinary circumstances was included in the handbook, there are broad regional differences, and that the regional offices—including the Gulf of Mexico Regional office—are continuing to develop internal

---

[52]GAO, *Offshore Oil and Gas Development: Additional Guidance Would Help Strengthen the Minerals Management Service's Assessment of Environmental Impacts in the North Aleutian Basin*, GAO-10-276 (Washington, D.C.: Mar. 8, 2010).

guidance that is more appropriately tailored to their specific geographical jurisdiction.

Since the *Deepwater Horizon* Incident, Use of Categorical Exclusions for Deepwater Plans Is Limited Pending Outcome of Internal Review

After the *Deepwater Horizon* incident, Interior limited its use of categorical exclusions to approve deepwater oil and gas activities in the Gulf of Mexico while it reviewed its NEPA policy and implemented a new requirement for preparing EA documents for exploration and development plans proposing deepwater projects. On August 16, 2010, the Council on Environmental Quality released a report on Interior's implementation of NEPA in its review and approval of exploration and development plans.[53,54] Among the report's findings was that Interior should (1) review its use of categorical exclusions for oil and gas exploration and development on the OCS in light of the increasing levels of complexity and risk and the potential environmental effects associated with deepwater drilling and (2) consider revising its policy for using categorical exclusions. The same day that the report was released, Interior announced that it was revising its categorical exclusion policy and, while certain shallow water drilling activities could still be approved using categorical exclusions, deepwater drilling activities could not, pending the outcome of an Interior review. On October 8, 2010, Interior published a notice in the *Federal Register* announcing its intent to conduct a broad review of its categorical exclusions for OCS decisions to ensure that it is in full compliance with NEPA and the regulations implementing NEPA.[55] Interior officials initially said that the report was to be completed in 2011 but that due to delays, it will not be finalized until mid-2012.

According to Interior officials, the new requirement to prepare EA documents for exploration and development plans for deepwater projects, instead of relying on categorical exclusions, has required additional time and resources for Interior's review but provides greater assurance that

---

[53]The Council on Environmental Quality coordinates federal environmental efforts and works closely with agencies and other White House offices in the development of environmental policies and initiatives. It was established within the Executive Office of the President by Congress as part of NEPA, and additional responsibilities were provided by the Environmental Quality Improvement Act of 1970.

[54]Council on Environmental Quality, *Report Regarding the Minerals Management Service's National Environmental Policy Act Policies, Practices, and Procedures as They Relate to Outer Continental Shelf Oil and Gas Exploration and Development* (Aug. 16, 2010).

[55]75 *Fed. Reg.* 62418 (2010).

environmental risks are considered. The officials stated that transitioning from categorical exclusions to site-specific EA documents for deepwater plans was initially challenging. For example, for exploration plans, staff had to produce a much more detailed and lengthy environmental analysis than previously required within the same 30-day review time frame. Interior officials reported that much of the initial difficulty in completing EA documents was getting the necessary information from the operator to complete the necessary analysis. Officials said that, going forward, they hope to streamline the EA process by developing a template that Interior staff can use to capture information to complete EA documents for exploration and development plans proposing projects in deepwater. Interior officials also reported that improving Interior's ability to prepare EA documents is contingent, in part, on acquiring additional staff.

Added Safety and Environmental Requirements for Exploration and Development Plans Appear to Have Initially Increased Exploration Plan Review Times, and Interior's TIMS IT System Hindered the Review Process

As previously discussed in this report, after the *Deepwater Horizon* incident, Interior enacted a number of policy changes to improve the safety of offshore oil and gas activities. In particular, Interior issued a Notice to Lessees and Operators, effective on June 18, 2010, that revised information requirements for exploration and development plans.[56] This guidance, in part, reversed a 2008 Notice to Lessees and Operators that limited the blowout scenario and worst case discharge information required to accompany such plans.[57] The new guidance required that operators submit more detailed information about their worst case discharge and blowout scenarios, along with information about how they would respond to a blowout. On August 16, 2010, Interior also issued a memorandum directing that all deepwater drilling plans be analyzed in EAs instead of through categorical exclusion reviews. These changes, according to Interior officials, would logically result in longer processing times for plans. However, according to Interior officials, Interior considered these changes necessary to ensure that operators provided sufficient environmental safeguards and projects received an appropriate level of NEPA review. Interior issued another Notice to Lessees and Operators effective about 5 months later on November 8, 2010, to inform

---

[56]NTL No. 2010-N06. Information Requirements for Exploration Plans, Development and Production Plans, and Development Operations Coordination Documents on the OCS. Effective on June 18, 2010.

[57]NTL No. 2008-G04. Information Requirements for Exploration Plans and Development Operations Coordination Documents. Effective on May 1, 2008.

operators that the agency would evaluate whether the operator's current oil spill response plan—typically examined during a review of an exploration or development plan—described the types and quantities of surface and subsea containment equipment that the operator could access in the event of a spill or threat of a spill and the deployment time.[58] Specifically, operators were encouraged to provide information in their oil spill response plans on well containment equipment such as capping stacks, dispersant systems, remotely operated underwater vehicles, and oil collection vessels, among other things, that would be necessary to respond to a subsea well blowout.

Our analysis of Interior's data from January 1, 2000, through September 30, 2011, suggest that after the *Deepwater Horizon* incident when new information requirements for exploration and development plans were implemented, plan review times and the number of amendments per plan initially generally increased. However, more recent data suggest that review times and amendments per plan have decreased somewhat, although not to levels prior to the incident. In addition, we found that Interior's TIMS IT system, which tracks amendments to plans, also hindered Interior's review.

Data Suggest Review Times and Frequency of Amendments Initially Generally Increased after New Safety and Environmental Requirements for Approved Exploration and Development Plans Were Enacted

Our analysis of Interior's data on review and approval of exploration and development plans suggests that, following the *Deepwater Horizon* incident and Interior's new safety and environmental requirements for plans, both review times and amendments per plan initially generally increased for approved plans when compared to before the incident. However, our analysis also suggests that, in some cases, review times and numbers of amendments per approved plan have recently decreased, although not to levels prior to the *Deepwater Horizon* incident. Specifically, our analysis of Interior's data from January 1, 2000, through September 30, 2011, found that after Interior added new requirements, the median review times initially increased for approved deepwater exploration and development plans and shallow water exploration plans but decreased for approved shallow water development plans. Amendments for both exploration and development plans irrespective of water depth initially increased. Interior officials stated that, over time, both review times and amendments may decrease as Interior staff and

---

[58]NTL No. 2010-N10. Statement of Compliance with Applicable Regulations and Evaluation of Information Demonstrating Adequate Spill Response and Well Containment Resources. Effective on November 8, 2010.

GAO-12-423 Oil and Gas Management

operators become more familiar with the new policy requirements. While our analysis of Interior's data suggest decreases in review times and numbers of amendments per plan, until several more years of post-*Deepwater Horizon* incident data are available, we can only present preliminary results of the effects of the new plan requirements on plan reviews.

We examined Interior's review of approved deepwater and shallow water exploration and development plans from initial submission to final approval for three time frames: (1) routine exploration and development plan reviews from January 1, 2000, through April 19, 2010; (2) a transition period when Interior staff and operators were adjusting to new policies—October 12, 2010, through May 31, 2011, for deepwater plans and June 8, 2010, through May 31, 2011, for shallow water plans; and (3) more recent reviews from June 1, 2011, through September 30, 2011.[59] Dividing the post-*Deepwater Horizon* incident period into two time frames allowed us to determine whether there had been a change in plan processing since the early post-*Deepwater Horizon* incident time frame and accompanying slowdown in reviews. Specifically, in dividing the post-*Deepwater Horizon* period into two time frames, we did not consider the outcome for any plan submitted in the first of these periods but approved in the second. Our methodology did not allow us to use data for plans that were submitted in either period but not approved prior to September 30, 2011. Therefore, we examined median processing times only for those plans that were both submitted and approved during a single one of these time frames and, as a result, some of our analysis was based on a small number of plans. Due to this limitation, our analysis should be viewed as provisional, awaiting the passage of time and the availability of additional data to allow for a more detailed examination of post-*Deepwater Horizon* incident plan processing times. It should also be noted that review times for exploration plans and development plans include both the time when plans are being reviewed at Interior and the time when plans are being revised by the applicant (in cases where an applicant's submission does not comply with regulatory requirements).

Deepwater exploration plans. Our analysis of Interior's data on deepwater exploration plans from January 1, 2000, through April 19,

---

[59]Our analysis did not examine review time frames for plans submitted from April 20, 2010, through June 7, 2010, for shallow water plans, and October 11, 2010, for deepwater plans, due to the effect of policy changes and the deepwater drilling moratorium.

2010, found that there were 1,374 plans submitted and approved within this time frame. These plans had a median review time of 38 days, and an average of 0.63 amendments per plan. For the policy transition period, from October 12, 2010, through May 31, 2011, our analysis found that there were 15 plans submitted and approved within this time frame. These plans had a median review time of 57 days and an average of 2.47 amendments per plan. For the last time frame, from June 1, 2011, through September 30, 2011, our analysis found that there were 5 plans that were submitted and approved within this time frame. These plans had median review time of 47 days and an average of 0.6 amendments per plan (see table 1).

Deepwater development plans. Our analysis of Interior's data on deepwater development plans from January 1, 2000, through April 19, 2010, found that there were 448 plans submitted and approved within this time frame. These plans had a median review time of 57 days and an average of 0.79 amendments per plan. For the policy transition period, from October 12, 2010, through May 31, 2011, our analysis found that that there were 16 plans submitted and approved within this time frame. These plans had a median review time of about 59.5 days and an average of 1.63 amendments per plan. For the last time frame, from June 1, 2011, through September 30, 2011, our analysis found that there were 7 plans submitted and approved within this time frame. These plans had a median review time of 56 days and an average of 0.86 amendments per plan (see table 1).

Table 1: Review Time Frames and Number of Amendments for Approved Deepwater Exploration and Development Plans from Initial Submission to Final Approval

	Exploration			Development		
	January 1, 2000, through April 19, 2010	October 12, 2010, through May 31, 2011	June 1, 2011, through September 30, 2011	January 1, 2000, through April 19, 2010	October 12, 2010, through May 31, 2011	June 1, 2011, through September 30, 2011
Total number of submittals with both initial plan submission date and plan approved date	1,374	15	5	448	16	7
Median days from initial plan submission to the plan approved date	38	57	47	57	59.5	56
Average number of amendments per approved plan	0.63	2.47	0.6	0.79	1.63	0.86

Source: GAO analysis of Interior data.

Shallow water exploration plans. Our analysis of Interior's data on shallow water exploration plans from January 1, 2000, through April 19, 2010, found that there were 1,982 plans submitted and approved within this time frame. These plans had a median review time of 39 days and an average of 0.54 amendments per plan. For the policy transition period, from June 8, 2010, through May 31, 2011, our analysis found that 14 were submitted and approved within this time frame. These plans had a median review time of 68 days and an average of 1.71 amendments per plan. For the last time frame, from June 1, 2011, through September 30, 2011, our analysis found that there were 3 plans submitted and approved within this time frame. These plans had a median review time of 51 days and an average of 0 amendments per plan.

Shallow water development plans. Our analysis of Interior's data on shallow water development plans from January 1, 2000, through April 19, 2010, found that 2,579 plans were submitted and approved within this time frame. These plans had a median review time of 43 days and an average of 0.47 amendments. For the policy transition period, from June 8, 2010, through May 31, 2011, our analysis found that that there were 39 plans submitted and approved within the time frame. These plans had a median review time of 39 days and an average of 1.79 amendments per plan. For the last time frame, from June 1, 2011, through September 30, 2011, our analysis found that there were 41 plans submitted and approved within the time frame. These plans had a median review time of 20 days and an average of 0.7 amendments per plan (see table 2).

GAO-12-423 Oil and Gas Management

Table 2: Review Time Frames and Number of Amendments for Approved Shallow Water Exploration and Development Plans from Initial Submission to Final Approval

	Exploration			Development		
	January 1, 2000, through April 19, 2010	June 8, 2010, through May 31, 2011	June 1, 2011, through September 30, 2011	January 1, 2000, through April 19, 2010	June 8, 2010, through May 31, 2011	June 1, 2011, through September 30, 2011
Total number of submittals with both initial plan submission date and plan approved date	1982	14	3	2579	39	41
Median days from initial plan submission to the plan approved date	39	68	51	43	39	20
Average number of amendments per approved plan	0.54	1.71	0	0.47	1.79	0.7

Source: GAO analysis of Interior data.

According to Interior officials, the new information requirements for exploration and development plans were confusing for both operators and Interior reviewers of those plans. As a result, operators amended plans more frequently, and the amendments added complexity to Interior's review process, increasing the time before Interior's final approval decision. Interior officials stated that amendments were often the result of errors or gaps in the information operators provided to Interior. Interior staff stated that, since the additional requirements went into effect, communication has increased between Interior and operators during the review process. For example, an Interior official told us that the policy change that led to the greatest increase in plan review times was the August 16, 2010, policy to complete EA documents for deepwater exploration or development plans instead of relying on categorical exclusions. As result of this new policy, Interior required additional information from operators in order to complete the EA documents. According to staff, this resulted in additional plan amendments, as operators were not initially submitting the necessary information, and led to overall increased review times. Additionally, Interior officials stated that the new policy requiring worst case discharge analyses was confusing for both operators and Interior and that the information and analyses operators initially provided were incorrect or incomplete and had to be amended. After approximately 6 months, however, Interior officials reported that they improved their ability to review the information and verify the calculations that operators provided and that operators gained a better understanding of how to complete the worst case discharge analysis in accordance with the new policy. Overall, Interior officials stated they expected that, as both staff and operators familiarize themselves with the new plan requirements, plan review times would decrease along with the number of plan amendments. After reviewing a draft of this report, Interior conducted its own analyses of plan review times using a different methodology and a longer time frame to show more recent trends. Similar to GAO's analysis, Interior found that review times have declined since the policy changes went into effect and the deepwater drilling moratorium was lifted. See appendix IV for additional details.

Interior's TIMS IT System Hindered Review of Plans

Interior officials reported that their review of exploration and development plans was further hindered by the limitations in its TIMS IT system including (1) no edit checks that would prevent operators from submitting incomplete and inaccurate plans, (2) no field to identify whether amendments to plans were made at the request of Interior or the operator, and (3) shortcomings in Interior's TIMS IT system for tracking plan amendments.

Interior has had a long-standing problem ensuring that operators submit complete and accurate plans, according to Interior officials, and developed a plan to address this limitation in 2003. According to Interior officials, Interior planned to develop an IT module called ePlans with data input controls—called edit checks—to limit operators' ability to submit incomplete or inaccurate plans and reduce the resources Interior invests in these reviews. However, ePlans was never completed due to cancellation by Interior in December 2010. As of September 2011, Interior officials reported they had worked with a consultant to develop a requirements document for procuring the ePlans module.

In addition, Interior officials stated that the TIMS IT system does not have a field for collecting information on whether amendments were submitted at the request of Interior to correct a deficiency or if the operator elected to revise its plan for technical reasons. As a result, when we attempted to analyze Interior's data to determine why plans were amended so frequently, we were unable to do so. Interior officials acknowledged that information on the reasons plans were amended would assist them to identify common deficiencies in plans that could be communicated to operators before they submit plans, potentially minimizing the number of incomplete or inaccurate plans. Despite the lack of an automated system to collect this data, Interior officials stated that they have identified common deficiencies in submitted plans and worked to communicate this information to operators on Interior's website and through plan workshops. Interior staff currently use a manual checklist for completeness, which Interior has shared with industry and the public through these workshops and on its website. According to Interior officials, this checklist will be incorporated into ePlans as Interior continues to develop the automated business rules and refine requirements for the system. Interior officials also stated that development of the ePlans system will depend on available funding through the budget process. However, without an automated system to identify deficiencies, Interior managers cannot readily determine if there are common deficiencies in operators' plans.

In addition, the limitations of Interior's TIMS IT system, which tracks plan amendments, makes it difficult for staff to identify the most current version of a plan. According to Interior officials, review staff were, at times, unsure which version was the most current, a problem that was exacerbated by new information requirements that generally increased the average number of amendments per plan. To address this issue, in June 2011, Interior officials began requesting that operators submit a composite plan—a complete, accurate, and final plan that includes all information from the initial plan and subsequent amendments. This composite plan would be submitted as the final amendment to the initial plan. While not a formal policy requirement, Interior officials stated that management communicated this new approach to Interior staff via e-mail, and staff, in turn, communicated it to operators by e-mail or telephone. Interior officials stated that once both Interior and operators become familiar with the new requirements for plans, the challenges staff currently face with amendments should decrease.

New Safety and Environmental Requirements for Drilling Permits Initially Increased Review Times

In addition to the new information requirements for exploration and development plans, Interior has added additional safety and environmental requirements for drilling permits designed to improve Interior's oversight of oil and gas drilling operations. Our analysis of Interior's new well and revised new well drilling permit review and approval data from January 1, 2005, through September 30, 2011, found that, after the new safety requirements went into effect, review times increased, as did the number of times that Interior returned a permit to an operator.

Interior Added Safety and Environmental Requirements for Drilling Permits

As previously discussed, Interior has issued a number of policy changes to enhance the safety of drilling operations on the OCS, including in the Gulf of Mexico. In particular, a June 8, 2010, Notice to Lessees and Operators outlined new requirements for obtaining drilling permits, as recommended by the Secretary of the Interior's May 2010 Safety

Measures Report. These new requirements include certification by the operator's Chief Executive Officer that operations were in compliance with Interior's regulations and third-party certifications of well design and the blowout preventer, among other things. On October 14, 2010, Interior incorporated some of these new safety requirements into an interim drilling safety rule, along with additional requirements intended to enhance the safety of drilling operations.[60] In issuing the interim drilling safety rule, Interior reported that "even without the full results of pending investigations, the obvious failures of well intervention and blowout containment systems demonstrate that previous regulatory assumptions concerning their reliability are inaccurate" and that the interim drilling safety rule "imposes requirements to give greater certainty that casing and cement design and fluid displacement are adequate for wellbore integrity, and to enhance the reliability of well control equipment." All together, Interior revised its drilling requirements related to well control, blowout preventers, well casing and cementing, secondary intervention, unplanned disconnects between drilling rigs and the blowout preventer, recordkeeping, well completion, and well plugging. Interior officials identified the following new safety requirements as the most significant:

Deepwater safety system requirement. Interior officials said that the new requirements for blowout preventers include testing specific components of the blowout preventer's emergency control systems. These systems are required for blowout preventers deployed on dynamically positioned drilling rigs[61] and, according to Interior officials, the new function testing requirements should provide greater assurance that emergency control systems will work in the event of, for example, an emergency disconnect between the rig and equipment located several thousand feet below on the seafloor.

Third-party verifications of blowout preventer components. Interior added a requirement for a third-party licensed entity to verify that the blind shear rams—the part of a blowout preventer that cuts the drill pipe and seals the well—have the capability to shear the drill pipe, by including

---

[60]Oil and Gas Sulfur Operations in the Outer Continental Shelf—Increased Safety Measures for Energy Development on the Outer Continental Shelf, 75 *Fed. Reg.* 63346 (2010), (amending 30 C.F.R. part 250).

[61]A dynamically positioned drilling rig is a drilling rig that is maintained in position over an offshore well location via thrusters, rather than mooring anchors.

shear test results and conducting calculations showing that the blowout preventer can shear the pipe under any condition.

Blowout preventer systems review. Interior now requires operators to submit additional schematics related to blowout preventers. According to Interior officials, Interior engineers now review each blowout preventer's schematics, including for anomalies. Interior officials told us that this increases the confidence that Interior understands how that particular blowout preventer works. According to Interior officials, should another incident similar to the *Deepwater Horizon* occur, it is critical that both Interior and the drilling rig contractor have the most up-to-date schematics of the blowout preventer. Officials explained that, during maintenance of blowout preventers, components, including hydraulic hoses, may be disconnected and reconnected. Without accurate schematics, neither Interior nor the operator would be able to identify whether the equipment was altered in a manner that could jeopardize its functioning. According to Interior officials, the *Deepwater Horizon* incident and the blowout preventer used for the well being drilled illustrate the importance of understanding how a blowout preventer works and the need for both Interior and the operator to have correct, up-to-date schematics. During the well blowout, the operator attempted repeatedly to activate one component of the blowout preventer to regain control of the well. However, because a hydraulic hose was installed incorrectly, the operator was unknowingly activating another component of the blowout preventer that was not designed to regain control and shut in the well.

Third-party certification of well casing design. Interior officials said this policy requires a certified engineer to review the well casing and certify that the design provides adequate well casing integrity. Interior officials pointed out, however, that a limitation of this policy requirement is that it does not require that a licensed petroleum engineer conduct the third-party review, only that the reviewer should be a professional engineer with a degree in any engineering position.

New standards for cement. Prior to the *Deepwater Horizon* incident, Interior officials stated that Interior's engineers reviewed a well permit's cement plan primarily to ensure that it included adequate volumes of cement to construct a safe and secure wellbore. Interior engineers did not, however, routinely consider the risks associated with the cementing plan. Interior's new requirement incorporates best practices for certain technical cementing,[62] which Interior officials said will provide greater assurance that the operator is examining any risks involved in its cementing plan.

Negative pressure test. Interior added new requirements specifying when an operator must conduct a negative pressure test—a test to verify the well is not capable of flow in the casing hole section being tested— and provide criteria for how it would successfully pass the test. Prior to the *Deepwater Horizon* incident and the recent interim final drilling safety rule, Interior officials told us that Interior did not have specific requirements for negative pressure tests. According to Interior officials, a negative pressure test lowers the pressure inside the wellbore to ensure that the casing and cement can withstand the pressure differential, separating the wellbore from the oil and gas reservoir. A blowout preventer is present during the test so that, if something goes wrong, it can be activated and prevent the release of oil or gas. According to an Interior official, failure to correctly interpret the negative pressure reading was likely a contributing factor to the well blowout in the *Deepwater Horizon* incident.

Data Suggest Drilling Permit Review Times and Permit Returns Initially Increased after New Safety and Environmental Requirements Were Enacted

Our analysis of Interior's data suggests that, as with the new requirements for exploration and development plans, Interior's drilling permit review times and permit returns generally increased after the *Deepwater Horizon* incident and Interior's new safety and environmental requirements for drilling permits intended to improve safety went into effect. However, our analysis also suggests that review times and numbers of returns per permit have decreased somewhat in the most recent time frame, although not to levels prior to the *Deepwater Horizon* incident. Specifically, our analysis of Interior's data from January 1, 2005, through September 30, 2011, found that after Interior added new requirements, the median review times initially increased for deepwater and shallow water new well and revised new well drilling permits. Returns per permit for both new well and revised new well permits, irrespective of water depth, also increased. Interior officials stated that, over time, both review times and returns per permit may decrease as Interior staff and

[62]Since the passage of the National Technology Transfer and Advancement Act in 1996, federal agencies have been required to adopt private-sector standards, which would include standards published by the American Petroleum Institute (API), wherever practical, in lieu of creating their own proprietary, nonconsensus standards. These best practices are based on API 65 part 2.

operators become more familiar with the new policy requirements. And while our analysis of Interior's data suggests decreases in review times and numbers of returns per permit, until several more years of post-*Deepwater Horizon* incident data available, we can only present preliminary results of the effects of the new permit requirements on permit reviews.

Similar to our analysis of Interior's reviews of exploration and development plans, we examined three distinct time frames for Interior's drilling permit reviews: (1) routine drilling permit review operations from January 1, 2005, through April 19, 2010;[63] (2) a transition period when Interior staff and operators were adjusting to new policies—October 12, 2010, through May 31, 2011, for deepwater drilling permits and June 8, 2010, through May 31, 2011, for shallow water drilling permits; and (3) recent drilling permit reviews from June 1, 2011, through September 30, 2011.[64] Dividing the post-*Deepwater Horizon* incident period into two time frames allowed us to determine whether there had been a change in permit processing since the early post-*Deepwater Horizon* incident time frame and accompanying slowdown in reviews. Specifically, in dividing the post-*Deepwater Horizon* period into two time frames, we did not consider the outcome for any permits submitted in the first of these time frames but approved in the second. Our methodology did not allow us to use data for permits that were submitted in either time frame but not approved prior to September 30, 2011. Therefore, we examined median processing times only for those permits that were both submitted and approved during a single one of these time frames and, as a result, some of our analysis was based on a small number of permits. Due to this limitation, our analysis should be viewed as provisional, awaiting the passage of time and the availability of additional data to allow a more detailed examination of post-*Deepwater Horizon* incident permit processing times. In addition to our analysis of new well and revised new well permits, we also examined permits for sidetracks, revised sidetracks, bypasses, and revised bypasses.

---

[63]Analysis of drilling permits prior to 2005 was not possible due to Interior officials' concerns about the reliability of the data.

[64]Our analysis did not examine review time frames for permits submitted from April 20, 2010, through June 7, 2010, for shallow water plans, and October 11, 2010, for deepwater plans, due to the effect of policy changes and the deepwater drilling moratorium.

Deepwater drilling permits. Our analysis of Interior's data on deepwater new well drilling permits from January 1, 2005, through April 19, 2010, found that 414 permits were submitted and approved within this time frame. These permits had a median review time of 20 days, and Interior returned the permits to the operator an average of about 1.57 times per permit. For the policy transition period, from October 12, 2010, through May 31, 2011, we found that 2 permits were submitted and approved within the time frame. These permits had a median review time of 68 days, and Interior returned the permits an average of 3.5 times per permit. For the most recent time frame—from June 1, 2011, through September 30, 2011—we found that 8 permits were submitted and approved within the time frame. These permits had a median review time of 32 days, and Interior returned the permits an average of 3 times per permit. See table 3 for information on all types of permits, including revised new wells, sidetracks, revised sidetracks, and bypasses.

Table 3: Review Time Frames and Average Number of Returns per Submission for All Types of Approved Deepwater Drilling Permits

	New well			Revised new well		
	January 1, 2005, through April 19, 2010	October 12, 2010, through May 31, 2011	June 1, 2011, through September 30, 2011	January 1, 2005, through April 19, 2010	October 12, 2010, through May 31, 2011	June 1, 2011, through September 30, 2011
Number of submittals approved	414	2	8	687	32	46
Median days from initial submittal until final approval	20	68	32	1	3.5	0.5
Average number of returned drilling permits per approved submittal	1.57	3.5	3	0.54	1.56	0.39

	Sidetrack			Revised sidetrack		
	January 1, 2005, through April 19, 2010	October 12, 2010, through May 31, 2011	June 1, 2011, through September 30, 2011	January 1, 2005, through April 19, 2010	October 12, 2010, through May 31, 2011	June 1, 2011, through September 30, 2011
Number of submittals approved	259	5	5	177	13	13
Median days from initial submittal until final approval	4	23	5	1	0	1
Average number of returned drilling permits per approved submittal	0.85	3.6	1	0.32	0.77	0.39

	Bypass			Revised bypass		
	January 1, 2005, through April 19, 2010	October 12, 2010, through May 31, 2011	June 1, 2011, through September 30, 2011	January 1, 2005, through April 19, 2010	October 12, 2010, through May 31, 2011	June 1, 2011, through September 30, 2011
Number of submittals approved	149	7	8	124	8	10
Median days from initial submittal until final approval	1	1	1.5	1	0.5	1.5
Average number of returned drilling permits per approved submittal	0.55	2.29	0.75	0.39	0.88	0.7

Source: GAO analysis of Interior data.

Shallow water drilling permits. Our analysis of Interior's drilling permit data from January 1, 2005, through April 19, 2010, for shallow water new well drilling permits found that 1,105 permits were submitted and approved within the time frame. These permits had a median review time of 11 days, and Interior returned the permits to the operator an average of 1.25 times per permit. For the policy transition period, from June 8, 2010, through May 31, 2011, we found that 43 permits were submitted and approved within the time frame. These permits had a median review time of 28 days, and Interior returned the permits an average of 2.37 times per permit. For the most recent time frame—from June 1, 2011, through September 30, 2011—we found that 18 permits were submitted and approved within the time frame. These permits had a median review time of 13.5 days, and Interior returned the permits an average of 2.11 times per permit. See table 4 for information on all types of permits, including revised new wells, sidetracks, revised sidetracks, and bypasses.

Table 4: Review Time Frames and Average Number of Returns per Submission for All Types of Approved Shallow Water Drilling Permits

	New well			Revised new well		
	January 1, 2005, through April 19, 2010	June 8, 2010, through May 31, 2011	June 1, 2011, through September 30, 2011	January 1, 2005, through April 19, 2010	June 8, 2010, through May 31, 2011	June 1, 2011, through September 30, 2011
Number of submittals approved	1,105	43	18	1,246	92	27
Median days from initial submittal until final approval	11	28	13.5	1	2	1
Average number of returned drilling permits per approved submittal	1.25	2.37	2.11	0.31	0.82	0.89

	Sidetrack			Revised sidetrack		
	January 1, 2005, through April 19, 2010	June 8, 2010, through May 31, 2011	June 1, 2011, through September 30, 2011	January 1, 2005, through April 19, 2010	June 8, 2010, through May 31, 2011	June 1, 2011, through September 30, 2011
Number of submittals approved	648	75	21	492	94	31
Median days from initial submittal until final approval	4	22	16	1	1	1
Average number of returned drilling permits per approved submittal	0.72	2.16	1.86	0.34	0.71	0.68

	Bypass			Revised bypass		
	January 1, 2005, through April 19, 2010	June 8, 2010, through May 31, 2011	June 1, 2011, through September 30, 2011	January 1, 2005, through April 19, 2010	June 8, 2010, through May 31, 2011	June 1, 2011, through September 30, 2011
Number of submittals approved	377	22	10	233	13	10
Median days from initial submittal until final approval	1	1	1	1	1	2
Average number of returned drilling permits per approved submittal	0.38	1.14	0.80	0.26	0.38	0.7

Source: GAO analysis of Interior data.

According to Interior officials, there has been a learning process for both Interior and operators as the new drilling safety requirements went into effect. At least one of the new requirements related to blowout preventers—reviewing the schematics—was initially difficult for Interior's engineers because, according to those officials, they did not have the expertise to review schematics. According to Interior officials, reviewing schematics involves printing the schematic, hanging it on a wall, and tracing every line on the blowout preventer to ensure that the blowout preventer is correctly configured. Interior staff reported that, after the first several blowout preventer schematic reviews, staff became more experienced. During their review of the schematics, Interior engineers found errors and notified the operators. In some instances, operators took up to 6 months to submit a corrected blowout preventer schematic to Interior. Interior officials reported that, prior to the *Deepwater Horizon* incident, there were 33 deepwater drilling rigs each with a subsea blowout preventer—typically the most complex blowout preventers that Interior reviews—deployed in the Gulf of Mexico. According to Interior officials, after Interior staff complete initial reviews of the remaining subsea blowout preventers, subsequent reviews should be more efficient because, if no changes are made to them, the operator may submit a statement certifying that no changes were made since Interior's last review. Interior officials added that Interior does not require a third-party certification of blowout preventer schematics as it does, for example, for the casing design.

Interior also reported mixed feedback from operators concerning the new drilling safety requirements. Interior officials told us that some operators stated that the requirements go beyond what is necessary to ensure the safety of offshore drilling, while others stated that the requirements are long overdue or expressed a desire to understand and comply with the new requirements. Despite the mixed feedback from operators, Interior officials expressed confidence that the new requirements would lead to greater safety for offshore drilling. Going forward, agency officials stated that drilling permit reviews should become more efficient as both Interior and operators become more familiar with the new requirements. After reviewing a draft of this report, Interior conducted its own analyses of permit review times using a different methodology and a longer time frame to show more recent trends. Similar to GAO's analysis, Interior found that review times have declined since the policy changes went into effect and the deepwater drilling moratorium was lifted. See appendix IV for additional details.

Inspections Routinely Identified Violations, and Policy Changes Are Under Way to Improve Inspection and Civil Penalty Programs

Interior's inspections of Gulf of Mexico offshore oil and gas drilling rigs and production platforms routinely identified violations from January 1, 2000, through September 30, 2011, but the inspection program faced several key challenges. Since the *Deepwater Horizon* incident, Interior has made policy changes to its inspection program to improve program oversight. Interior issued approximately $18 million in civil penalty assessments during this period, and district managers generally agreed with inspection staff recommendations to formally open civil penalty cases. Since the incident, Interior also made policy changes to improve its civil penalty program.

Interior's Inspection Program Routinely Identified Violations but Was Hindered by Three Key Challenges

Our analysis of Interior's inspection data from January 1, 2000, through September 30, 2011,[65] found that approximately 8 percent of drilling rig inspections and 28 percent of production platform inspections identified violations. However, three key challenges hindered Interior's inspection program: (1) Interior did not generally meet its informal goal for conducting monthly drilling rig inspections, (2) Interior did not have a formal policy for conducting announced versus unannounced inspections

---

[65]Because the *Deepwater Horizon* incident was a unique event, inspection data presented for 2010 may not be representative of normal Interior operations.

until fiscal year 2012, and (3) Interior was missing about half of the data on whether violations it identified were corrected.

Drilling rig inspection rates and violations. Our analysis of Interior's data on drilling rig inspection rates—the number of days a drilling rig was on site divided by the number of inspections per month—indicates that Interior met its informal drilling rig inspection goal in 1 of 11 years for the period from January 1, 2000, through 2010,[66] but it appeared likely to meet its goal for 2011. The OCS Lands Act requires Interior to conduct annual inspections for all offshore structures, and Interior, according to Interior officials, developed an informal goal of inspecting active drilling rigs monthly, which was never formalized in documented policy. During the period of our analysis, the overall number of drilling rig inspections generally declined from 2,208 in 2000 to 771 in 2009—the last calendar year for which complete data were available prior to the *Deepwater Horizon* incident; the decline was largely the result of reduced drilling activity in the Gulf of Mexico, according to Interior officials. During this same time period, the average drilling rig inspection rate varied from a high of 1.15 per month in 2000 to a low of 0.61 per month in 2008 (see fig. 8). According to Interior officials, Interior may be even less likely to consistently meet this informal goal in future years for several reasons. First, as oil and gas drilling activities move further offshore to develop deepwater projects, travel times for inspections will increase, thereby increasing the average time per inspection. Second, new safety requirements Interior issued require operators to notify Interior at least 72 hours before blowout preventer testing to facilitate having Interior inspection staff present to witness at least one of the tests. These new requirements have required inspectors to remain on drilling rigs for several days, thereby lengthening the time for each drilling rig inspection. Additionally, inspection frequency can be greatly affected by weather, especially in the winter months. Fog, high winds, and severe storms can prevent inspectors from conducting inspections for many days. Nonetheless, Interior continues to rely on its informal goal for inspecting drilling rigs and has not assessed how new policy requirements and travel times to deepwater drilling rigs would affect its ability to conduct these monthly drilling rig inspections.

---

[66]Our analysis determined the drilling rig inspection rate by dividing the number of active rig days on location by the number of inspections per 30 days. This analysis does not indicate whether each drilling rig was inspected once every 30 days.

Our analysis of drilling rig inspections found that the percentage of violations associated with drilling rig inspections remained within a small range during the period of our analysis. Specifically, from 2000 through 2010, the percentage of inspections associated with violations ranged from 5 percent to 10 percent. However, data for the first 9 months of 2011 indicate that over 19 percent of drilling rig inspections were associated with violations, the highest percentage we found (see fig. 8).

Figure 8: Drilling Rig Inspections, Violations, and Inspections per 30 Days, January 1, 2000, through September 30, 2011

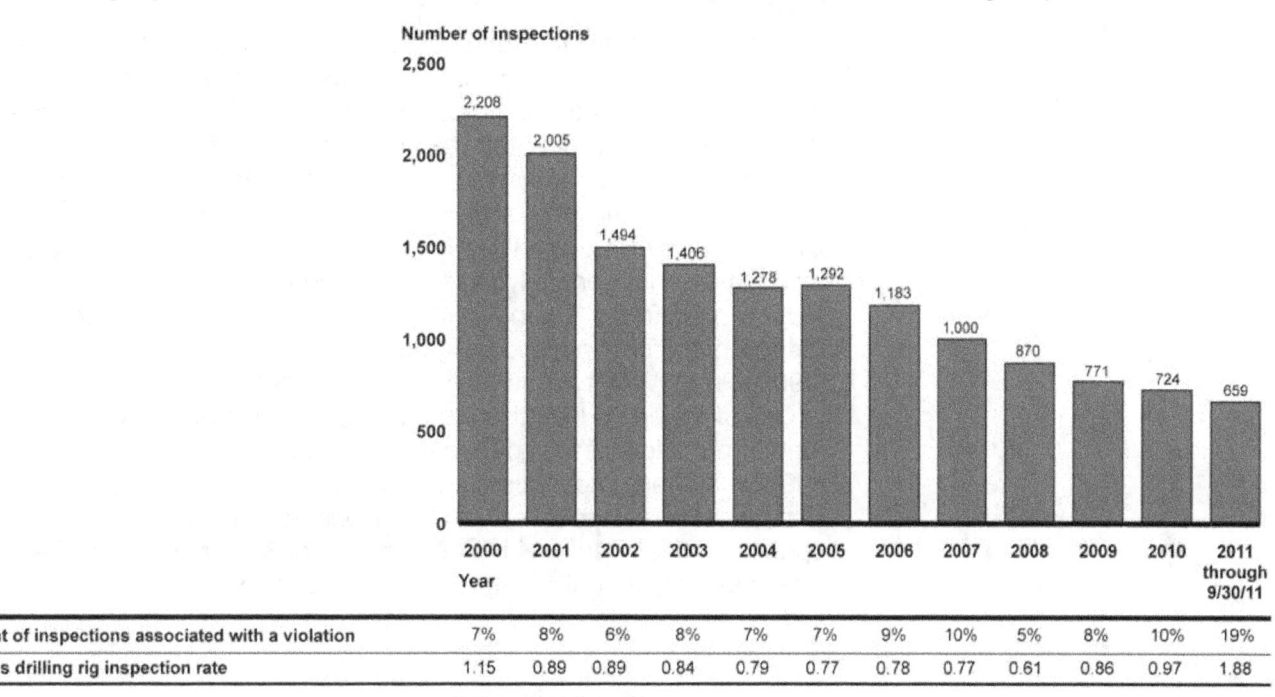

	2000	2001	2002	2003	2004	2005	2006	2007	2008	2009	2010	2011 through 9/30/11
Percent of inspections associated with a violation	7%	8%	6%	8%	7%	7%	9%	10%	5%	8%	10%	19%
30-days drilling rig inspection rate	1.15	0.89	0.89	0.84	0.79	0.77	0.78	0.77	0.61	0.86	0.97	1.88

Source: GAO analysis of Interior data.

Note: Because the *Deepwater Horizon* incident was a unique event, data presented for 2010 may not be representative of normal Interior operations.

When examining all categories of violations associated with drilling rigs during this period, we found that the 10 most frequent violations fell into three of Interior's violation categories: (1) general operations, (2) drilling operations, and (3) pollution events. Specifically, 5 of the 10 most frequent violations were related to general operations,[67] 3 were related to drilling operations, and 2 were related to pollution events.[68] Overall, the most frequent violation was in general operations—for example, the inspector observed that the operator was not performing operations in a "workmanlike manner," among other criteria. In this case, a violation could be issued if, for example, an inspector saw tools or other equipment lying on the ground that could pose a safety hazard for other workers on the rig. Other frequent violations for drilling operations were related to technical deficiencies in testing blowout preventers.

Production platform inspection rates and violations. Our analysis of Interior's data on production platform inspection rates—the number of production platforms divided by the number of inspections per year— indicates that Interior generally exceeded its goal of annually inspecting production platforms for the 11 years from January 1, 2000, through 2010,[69] but it was uncertain whether it would meet its goal for 2011. When examining Interior's oil and gas production platform inspection data, we found that Interior generally exceeded its goal of annually inspecting production platforms. During the period of our analysis, the number of production platform inspections generally declined from 4,249 in 2000 to 3,390 in 2010. When accounting for the number of production platforms in the Gulf of Mexico during this period, Interior's average inspection rate ranged from a low of 1.03 per year in 2007 to a high of 1.29 per year in 2009. On average, approximately 28 percent of production platform inspections were associated with violations, ranging from a low of approximately 20 percent in 2008 to a high of 34 percent in 2010—a rate higher than that for drilling rig inspections (see fig. 9).

---

[67]General operation violations include violations related to accident reporting and record keeping.

[68]Pollution event violations include violations related to pollution prevention and oil spill reports.

[69]Our analysis determined the production platform inspection rate by dividing the number of production platforms by the number of inspections per year. This analysis does not indicate whether each production platform was inspected once per year.

Figure 9: Production Platform Inspections, Violations, and Annual Inspections per Production Platform, January 1, 2000, through September 30, 2011

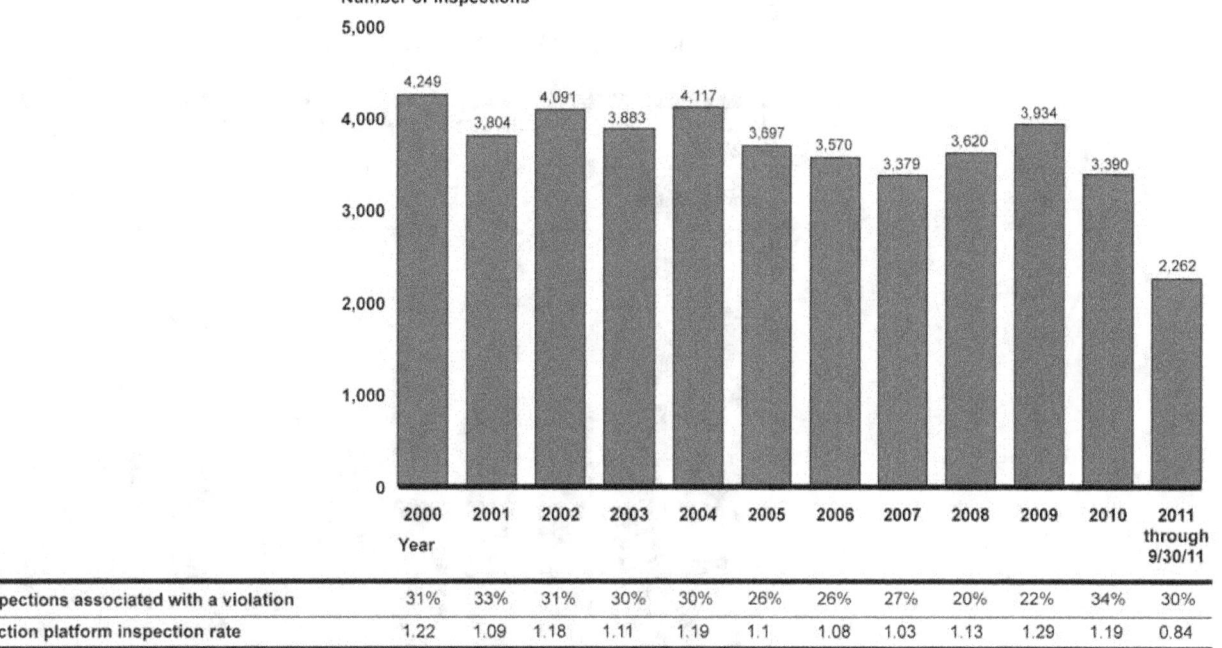

Percent of inspections associated with a violation	31%	33%	31%	30%	30%	26%	26%	27%	20%	22%	34%	30%
Annual production platform inspection rate	1.22	1.09	1.18	1.11	1.19	1.1	1.08	1.03	1.13	1.29	1.19	0.84

Source: GAO analysis of Interior data.

Note: Because the *Deepwater Horizon* incident was a unique event, data presented for 2010 may not be representative of normal Interior operations.

When examining all categories of violations associated with production platforms during this period, similar to drilling rigs, we found that the 10 most frequent violations fell into 3 categories: (1) production operations, (2) general operations, and (3) pollution events. Specifically, 5 of the 10 most frequent violations were related to production operations, 4 were related to general operations, and 1 was related to a pollution event. Similar to drilling rig inspections, the most frequently issued violations were related either to inspectors observing unsafe work practices or unsafe conditions.

Enforcement actions. We found that the severity of Interior's enforcement actions in response to about half of all drilling rig and production platform violations issued from January 1, 2000, through September 30, 2011, were warnings, and the other half resulted in orders to either shut down the component in violation—such as a piece of equipment—or, if sufficiently serious, shut down the entire drilling rig or production platform. Specifically, our analysis of drilling rig enforcement actions from January 1, 2000, through September 30, 2011, found that, on average, approximately 60 percent of the violations were warnings, 20 percent were component or well shut down orders, and 20 percent were drilling rig shutdown orders (see fig. 10).

Figure 10: Drilling Rig Enforcement Actions, January 1, 2000, through September 30, 2011

Percent of violations

Year	2000	2001	2002	2003	2004	2005	2006	2007	2008	2009	2010	2011 through 9/30/11
Number of violations	259	305	134	166	119	153	244	154	72	114	113	211

☐ Violations leading to a shutdown of a component or well

▨ Violations leading to a shutdown of an entire structure

■ Violations leading to a warning

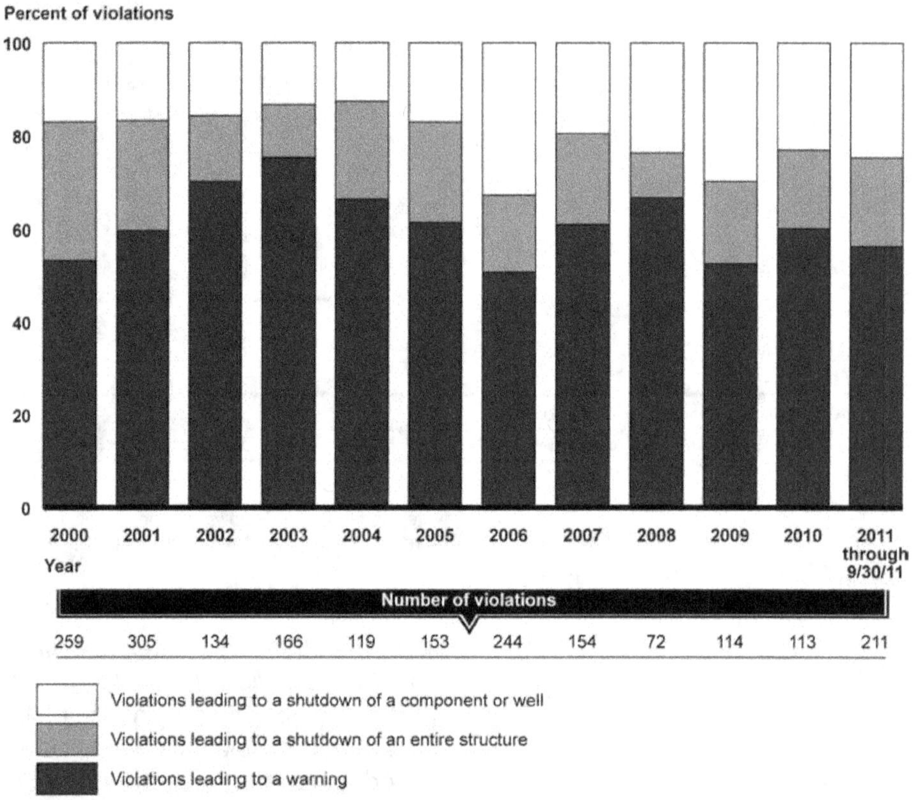

Source: GAO analysis of Interior data.

Note: Because the *Deepwater Horizon* incident was a unique event, data presented for 2010 may not be representative of normal Interior operations.

Our analysis of production platform enforcement actions from January 1, 2000, through September 30, 2011, showed that, on average, approximately 50 percent of the violations were warnings, 46 percent were component or well shutdown requests, and about 4 percent were production platform shutdown requests (see fig. 11).

Figure 11: Production Platform Enforcement Actions, January 1, 2000, through September 30, 2011

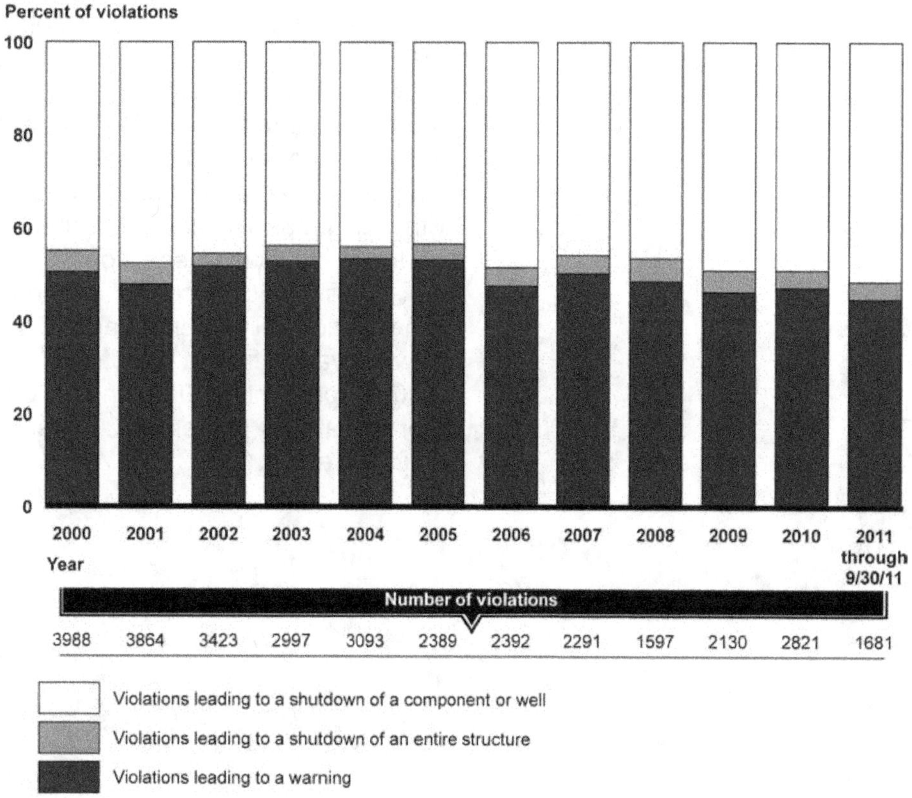

Percent of violations

Year	2000	2001	2002	2003	2004	2005	2006	2007	2008	2009	2010	2011 through 9/30/11
Number of violations	3988	3864	3423	2997	3093	2389	2392	2291	1597	2130	2821	1681

☐ Violations leading to a shutdown of a component or well

▨ Violations leading to a shutdown of an entire structure

■ Violations leading to a warning

Source: GAO analysis of Interior data.

Note: Because the *Deepwater Horizon* incident was a unique event, data presented for 2010 may not be representative of normal Interior operations.

Interior officials explained that the financial cost incurred by the operator associated with shutting down a production platform or drilling rig can be significant. However, officials explained that the operator may be able to correct the violation while the inspector is present, meaning that the component or the production platform or drilling rig is not shut down. For example, an operator may forget to open a safety valve after an equipment test, which could result in a violation, as well as a mandatory shut down of the production platform or drilling rig. However, since the operator can immediately fix the problem, the facility would not be shut down, but would still receive a violation.

GAO-12-423 Oil and Gas Management

Announced versus unannounced inspections. Interior has authority to conduct both announced and unannounced inspections, but did not have a documented policy to differentiate between them until fiscal year 2012. For both drilling rigs and production platforms, we found that unannounced inspections were associated with a greater number of violations than were announced inspections from January 1, 2000, through September 30, 2011. For example, we found that about 8 percent of announced drilling rig inspections were associated with violations compared to about 10 percent of unannounced inspections associated with violations. Similarly, we found that 28 percent of announced production platform inspections were associated with violations, whereas approximately 45 percent of unannounced inspections were associated with violations. The percentage of unannounced inspections of drilling rigs per year varied from a low of zero percent in 2002 and 2003 to a high of about 11 percent in 2009, and for production platforms, from a low of approximately 1 percent in 2008 and 2009 to a high of about 11 percent in 2000 (see fig. 12).

Figure 12: Announced and Unannounced Inspections and Associated Violations, January 1, 2000, through September 30, 2011

	Drilling rigs			Production platforms		
	Percentage of inspections			Percentage of inspections		
	All inspections		Associated with a violation	All inspections		Associated with a violation
2000	95% / 5%	Unannounced	8%	89% / 11%	Unannounced	30%
		Announced	7%		Announced	32%
2001	98% / 2%	Unannounced	5%	93% / 7%	Unannounced	38%
		Announced	9%		Announced	33%
2002	100% / 0%	Unannounced	0%	94% / 6%	Unannounced	34%
		Announced	6%		Announced	31%
2003	100% / 0%	Unannounced	0%	95% / 5%	Unannounced	41%
		Announced	8%		Announced	30%
2004	95% / 5%	Unannounced	6%	96% / 4%	Unannounced	33%
		Announced	7%		Announced	30%
2005	92% / 8%	Unannounced	11%	96% / 4%	Unannounced	27%
		Announced	7%		Announced	26%
2006	90% / 10%	Unannounced	16%	97% / 3%	Unannounced	42%
		Announced	8%		Announced	25%
2007	93% / 7%	Unannounced	15%	97% / 3%	Unannounced	35%
		Announced	9%		Announced	27%
2008	91% / 9%	Unannounced	7%	99% / 1%	Unannounced	35%
		Announced	5%		Announced	19%
2009	89% / 11%	Unannounced	8%	99% / 1%	Unannounced	28%
		Announced	8%		Announced	22%
2010	92% / 8%	Unannounced	7%	98% / 2%	Unannounced	46%
		Announced	10%		Announced	32%
2011 through 9/30/11	93% / 7%	Unannounced	19%	94% / 6%	Unannounced	40%
		Announced	19%		Announced	29%
Total/average		Unannounced 5%	10%		Unannounced 5%	45%
		Announced 95%	8%		Announced 95%	28%

Source: GAO analysis of Interior data.

Note: Because the *Deepwater Horizon* incident was a unique event, data presented for 2010 may not be representative of normal Interior operations.

GAO-12-423 Oil and Gas Management

Interior officials told us that conducting unannounced inspections can be logistically challenging for several reasons. For example, without advance notice to the drilling rig or production platform, Interior may have difficulty landing a helicopter because the landing pad on the rig or platform may be occupied by another helicopter, or operators may be actively using a crane to move equipment, which prevents a safe landing. Additionally, without advance scheduling, the operator may not have all of the personnel available that the inspectors need to meet with to conduct the inspection. Moreover, according to Interior officials, the resources necessary to conduct annual announced inspections required under the OCS Lands Act does not allow Interior inspectors much time to conduct unannounced inspections. Interior officials stated that as more inspection staff are hired and trained, they expect to conduct greater numbers of unannounced inspections. Recently, Interior issued guidance to each of its district offices informing them of the number of unannounced inspections—including inspections of drilling rigs—required to be conducted in fiscal year 2012.[70] Specifically, each of the five district offices in the Gulf of Mexico is required to conduct unannounced inspections of 15 percent of all manned platforms or drilling rigs within their district.

Violation correction dates. We also found that Interior did not record in its TIMS IT system whether about half of the violations issued from January 1, 2000, through September 30, 2011, were ever corrected, raising questions about the safety of offshore oil and gas operations. According to Interior's policy, operators generally have 14 days to respond to an issued violation. The operator is required to mail Interior a copy of the violation along with steps taken by the operator to correct the violation or request an extension for correcting the violation. According to Interior officials, paper copies of this information should be retained in Interior's files and subsequently keyed into Interior's electronic database. However, when examining Interior's data, we found that from January 1, 2000, through September 30, 2011, violation correction dates were missing from Interior's TIMS IT system for a significant number of violations of varying levels of enforcement action. For example, for the period examined, approximately 58 percent of warning violations were missing a correction date, as were 42 percent of component shutdown

---

[70]According to Interior's policy, the definition of an unannounced inspection is one that is performed without prior notification; that is, the operator shall be notified only 20 minutes before landing on the facility.

violations and 44 percent of drilling rig or production platform shutdown violations. According to the standards for internal control in the federal government, agencies are to promptly record transactions and events to maintain their relevance to management in controlling operations and making decisions.[71] Interior officials stated that they were uncertain why violation correction data was not consistently being entered into the TIMS IT system. Moreover, one official told us that, in some cases, violation data is entered into the TIMS IT system only after the violation is corrected. Because Interior is not recording data in an accurate and consistent manner, Interior management does not know on a real-time basis whether or when violations were identified or corrected, potentially allowing unsafe activities to continue (see fig. 13).

Figure 13: Missing Violation Correction Data by Severity of Violation, January 1, 2000, through September 30, 2011

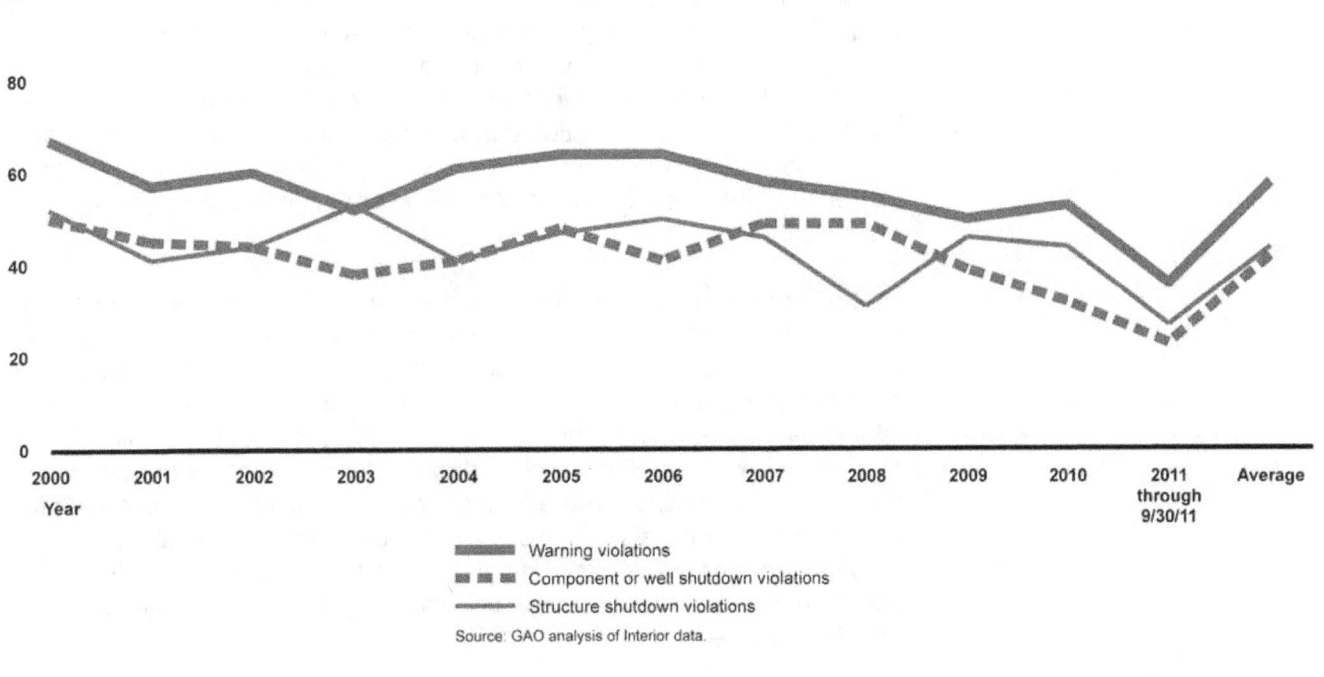

Percentage of violations missing correction data

Warning violations
Component or well shutdown violations
Structure shutdown violations

Source: GAO analysis of Interior data.

[71]GAO, *Standards for Internal Control in the Federal Government*, GAO/AIMD-00-21.3.1 (Washington, D.C.: November 1999).

Policy Changes Intended to Improve Inspection Program Are Under Way

Interior officials stated that numerous efforts and policy changes are under way to improve Interior's inspection program in the aftermath of the *Deepwater Horizon* incident, including (1) hiring additional inspectors, (2) considering specialization of inspection staff, (3) shifting from one-person to two-person inspection teams, (4) requiring additional documentation of inspections, and (5) requiring that inspectors witness blowout preventer tests. Interior has not, however, expanded a 2009 voluntary pilot program whereby inspection staff could electronically access and review operators' records while onshore, allowing additional time to physically inspect operations when offshore on a production platform or drilling rig.

Hiring inspectors. Interior determined that its inspection staff was too small and not sufficient to carry out its new oversight responsibilities. Since the *Deepwater Horizon* incident, Interior officials told us that, as of March 2012, they hired 43 new Gulf of Mexico region inspectors while losing 24, resulting in a net increase of 19 inspectors. Additionally, in April 2011, Interior reported it was creating a new training program for its inspection staff. According to the new national training director, it may be up to 2 years before new inspection staff are fully trained under the new training program, meaning that while the number of inspectors has increased, Interior's inspection capacity has not necessarily increased commensurately. However, Interior has not assessed how the numbers of inspectors hired would affect its ability to conduct monthly drilling rig inspections.

Specialization of inspectors. As of December 2011, Interior's inspection staff did not specialize in specific offshore activities, such as oil and gas measurement, drilling, or well abandonment. However, Interior officials reported that, given the complexity of the operations occurring, they are initiating an inspection program whereby inspection staff specialize in technical aspects of offshore oil and gas activities, such as drilling, with the goal of conducting more effective and robust oversight. According to several Interior officials, a more specialized inspection workforce would result in more effective oversight. However, this effort is closely linked with its newly established formal training program and the ability to hire additional inspectors.

Inspection teams. In June 2011, Interior announced that it planned to begin using multiple person teams to conduct inspections. Several Interior officials stated that this approach should result in better oversight, but in the short term, overall inspection numbers may temporarily decline because moving from a one-person inspection team to two-person inspection teams will decrease the number of inspections in which each inspector can participate in.

Documentation of inspections. Prior to the *Deepwater Horizon* incident, Interior inspection staff did not always document what they examined during inspections. According to several Interior officials, Interior historically required inspectors to use a checklist to document their inspections, but as inspection staff became more experienced over the past 10 years, Interior stopped requiring such documentation. Since the *Deepwater Horizon* incident, Interior officials told us that Interior has again begun to require that inspectors document that all aspects of an inspection were completed. Additionally, beginning in July 2011, Interior began training inspectors for a pilot program using laptops, as opposed to paper records, to document drilling inspections while offshore on a drilling rig. According to an Interior official, the pilot program is an electronic-based documentation system that provides inspectors with all of the data they need to perform an inspection, including the inspection form in electronic format.

Witnessing blowout preventer tests. As a result of the new safety requirements, inspection staff are to witness blowout preventer tests to better ensure that blowout preventers will work when needed. According to Interior officials, these new inspections can take a long time because of the difficulty coordinating the timing of a blowout preventer test with an operator. As a result, inspectors may remain on a drilling rig for several days waiting for the operator to complete the test, which prevents the inspector from completing inspections on other drilling rigs or production platforms.

Pilot program for electronic inspections of records. In 2008, Interior implemented a pilot program called eInspection—a program that allows operators to upload certain records related to oil and gas measurement to an electronic database and enable inspectors to review the records electronically from onshore, for example, on days when weather prevents them from flying to drilling rigs or production platforms offshore. According to an Interior official, while this program is still ongoing, it has not had much participation from industry. To date, Interior has not implemented similar programs for other types of inspections, such as drilling. Gulf of Mexico region officials stated that improvements to eInspection could significantly improve the use of agency and operator resources and reduce costs. Specifically, they cited benefits such as (1) maintaining productivity during bad weather; (2) limiting the number of expensive helicopter flights; (3) improving inspection efficiencies through the division of inspection duties; and (4) allowing Interior to retain experienced staff that can no longer meet the physical requirements for conducting offshore inspections, such as periodic helicopter crash simulation training. Some Interior officials cautioned that, despite the potential benefits of this program, its expansion to other types of inspections would likely require new regulations and could pose challenges for smaller operators that might not currently store their records electronically.

Violations Resulted in $18 Million in Civil Penalty Assessments

Our analysis of Interior data showed that from January 1, 2000, through September 30, 2011, Interior issued approximately $18 million in civil penalty assessments for violations associated with drilling rigs and production platforms.[72] During this period, inspectors referred violations for consideration to formally open a civil penalty case, and Interior district managers agreed with over 50 percent of inspectors' referrals. Once a civil penalty case was officially opened, most led to an assessment, which took an average of 213 days to bring the case to resolution.

Violations associated with civil penalty assessments. We reviewed Interior's data on civil penalty assessments for violations associated with drilling rigs and production platforms from January 1, 2000, through September 30, 2011, and found that Interior issued about $18 million in civil penalty assessments for such violations. Of this $18 million, about $2 million was assessed for drilling rig violations and $16 million for production platform violations. Tables 5 and 6 show the number of total violations, those violations that were assessed with civil penalties, and the dollar amounts of those assessments for drilling rigs and production platforms, respectively.

---

[72]All civil penalty assessments are presented in nominal dollars.

Table 5: Civil Penalties Associated with All Drilling Rig Violations, January 1, 2000, through September 30, 2011

Year	Drilling rig violations	Drilling rig violation not associated with civil penalty	Drilling rig violation associated with civil penalty	Total amount of civil penalties assessed
2000	259	251	8 (3 %)	$116,000
2001	305	301	4 (1 %)	$102,000
2002	134	127	7 (5 %)	$190,000
2003	166	165	1 (1 %)	$25,000
2004	119	114	5 (4 %)	$60,000
2005	153	148	5 (3 %)	$268,000
2006	244	203	41 (17 %)	$673,500
2007	154	148	6 (4 %)	$242,000
2008	72	68	4 (6 %)	$40,000
2009	114	105	9 (8 %)	$210,000
2010	113	109	4 (4 %)	$115,000
2011[a]	211	206	5 (2 %)	
Total	**2,044**	**1,945**	**99 (5 %)**	**$2,041,500**

Source: GAO analysis of Interior data.

[a]Data for 2011 are through September 30, 2011.

Table 6: Civil Penalties Associated with Production Platform Violations, January 1, 2000, through September 30, 2011

Year	Production platform violations	Production platform violation not associated with civil penalty	Production platform violation associated with civil penalty	Total amount of civil penalties assessed
2000	3,988	3,863	125 (3 %)	$2,569,000
2001	3,864	3,700	164 (4 %)	$1,520,450
2002	3,423	3,349	74 (2 %)	$1,612,450
2003	2,997	2,975	22 (1 %)	$707,250
2004	3,093	3,036	57 (2 %)	$802,500
2005	2,389	2,339	50 (2 %)	$961,500
2006	2,392	2,293	99 (4 %)	$2,154,500
2007	2,291	2,247	44 (2 %)	$2,167,750
2008	1,597	1,561	36 (2 %)	$529,000
2009	2,130	2,096	34 (2 %)	$1,963,000
2010	2,821	2,776	45 (2 %)	$1,346,250
2011[a]	1,689	1,646	43 (3 %)	$95,000
Total	**32,674**	**31,881**	**793 (2 %)**	**$16,428,650**

Source: GAO analysis of Interior data.

[a]Data for 2011 are through September 30, 2011.

Interior may assess civil penalties at a daily rate, and such penalties can accrue over time. For example, Interior may impose a single $40,000 civil penalty assessment for a serious violation or a $5,000 per-day civil penalty assessment for a less serious violation, resulting in a $40,000 fine if the operator took 8 days to correct the violation. According to Interior officials, data on civil penalty assessments—by day and by violation—would be useful in examining civil penalty trends over time. However, Interior's TIMS IT system does not contain the data in a way that would allow program managers to identify trends in the civil penalty program. Because Interior management cannot readily distinguish whether civil penalties were more frequently associated with significant violations that were immediately corrected, as opposed to less serious violations that were not immediately corrected, its ability to examine civil penalty trends over time is limited.

Violation referrals for civil penalty case consideration. In examining Interior's civil penalty data from January 1, 2000, through September 30, 2011, we found that Interior's district managers agreed with inspection staffs' recommendations to develop a violation for civil penalty review about 56 percent of the time. According to Interior officials, when inspection staff refer a violation for consideration for civil penalties, both the district supervisory inspector and district manager review the violation to verify that it meets the specified criteria for officially opening a civil penalty case. Ultimately, the district manager determines whether to officially develop a civil penalty case and forward the information to the civil penalty case reviewing officer. Our analysis of Interior's civil penalty data found that inspection staff referred 1,439 violations for consideration for civil penalties and that district managers agreed with inspectors for 802 of these violations, or about 56 percent of the violations (see fig. 14).

Figure 14: Violations Flagged for Civil Penalty Consideration and District Manager Review, January 1, 2000, through September 30, 2011

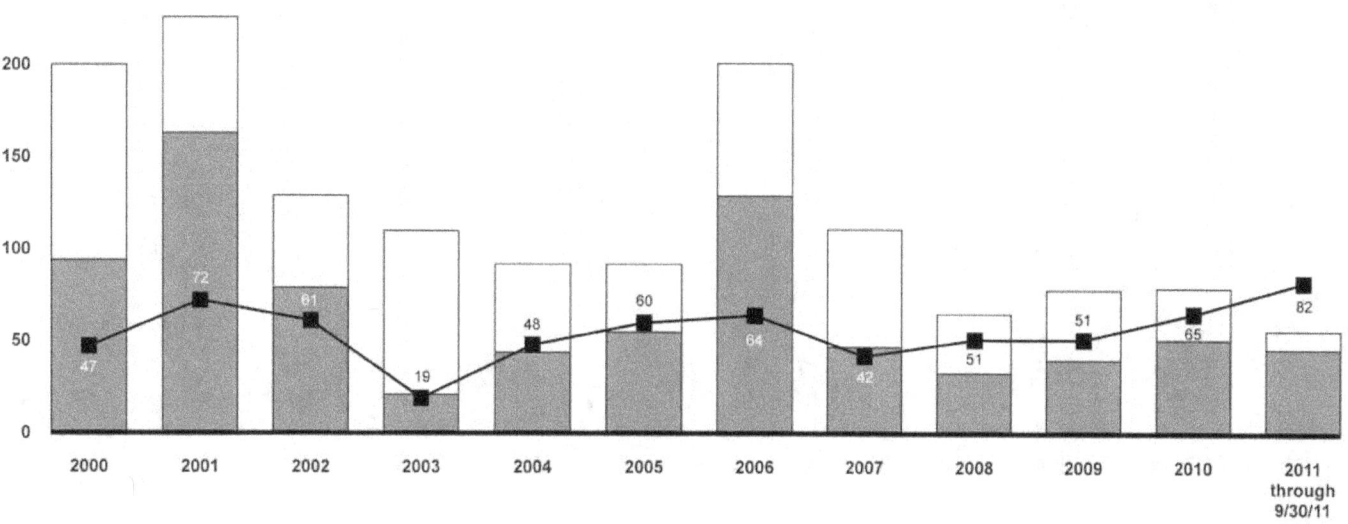

Number of violations

Inspection year

District manager disagreed with inspector recommendation to initiate civil penalty review

District manager agreed with inspector recommendation to initiate civil penalty review

Percent of violations where district manager agreed with inspector to develop a civil penalty case

Source: GAO analysis of Interior data.

Violations leading to civil penalty assessments. Our analysis found that once a district manager determined that a violation warranted consideration for a civil penalty assessment, Interior assessed a civil penalty in approximately 89 percent of these violations from January 1, 2000, through September 30, 2011. Specifically, we found that of the 1,232 violations considered for a civil penalty assessment, Interior assessed a civil penalty for 1,099 violations, or about 89 percent of the time (see fig. 15). Interior officials reported that during the time when a civil penalty reviewing officer develops the case, the reviewing officer may decide not to assess a civil penalty based on the available evidence.

Figure 15: Violations Considered for a Civil Penalty Assessment and Whether a Civil Penalty Was Assessed, January 1, 2000, through September 30, 2011

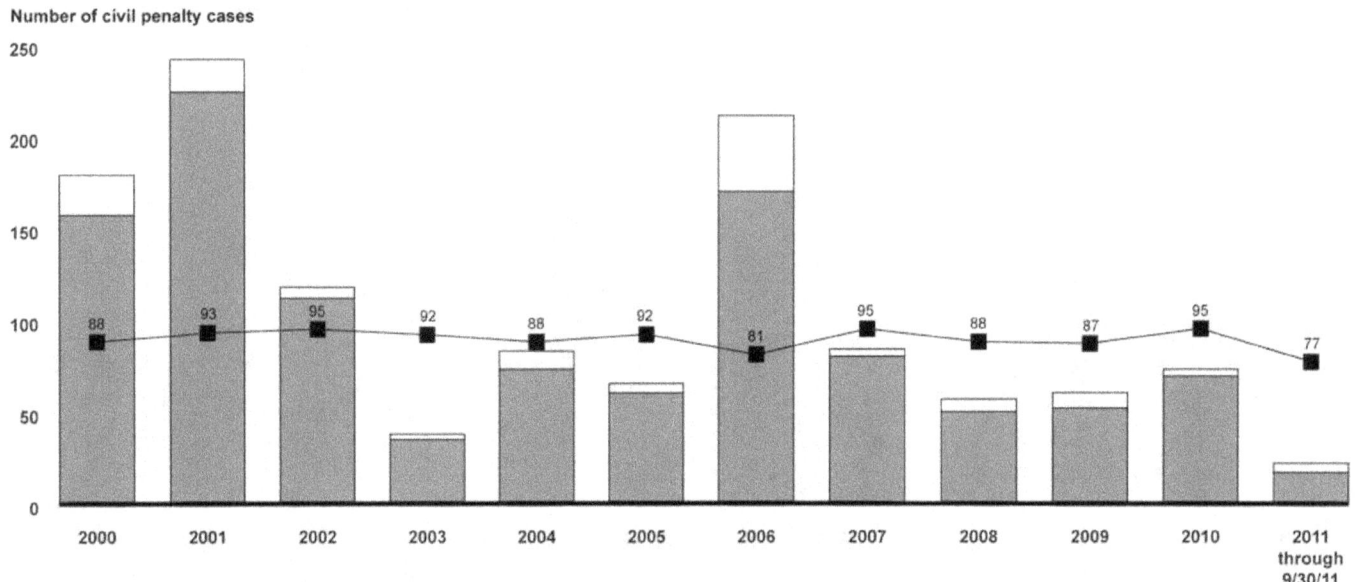

Source: GAO analysis of Interior data.

Duration of civil penalty cases. For the period reviewed, once a civil penalty case was officially opened, Interior spent an average of 213 days to bring the case to resolution. The days to complete a civil penalty review varied from a high of 323 days in 2003 to a low of 119 days in 2011, with a slight overall decline over time. Interior officials told us that the length of time to complete a review is a concern for them, and that they are planning to examine how to shorten the duration of civil penalty cases going forward (see fig. 16).

Figure 16: Duration of Civil Penalty Cases, January 1, 2000, through September 30, 2011

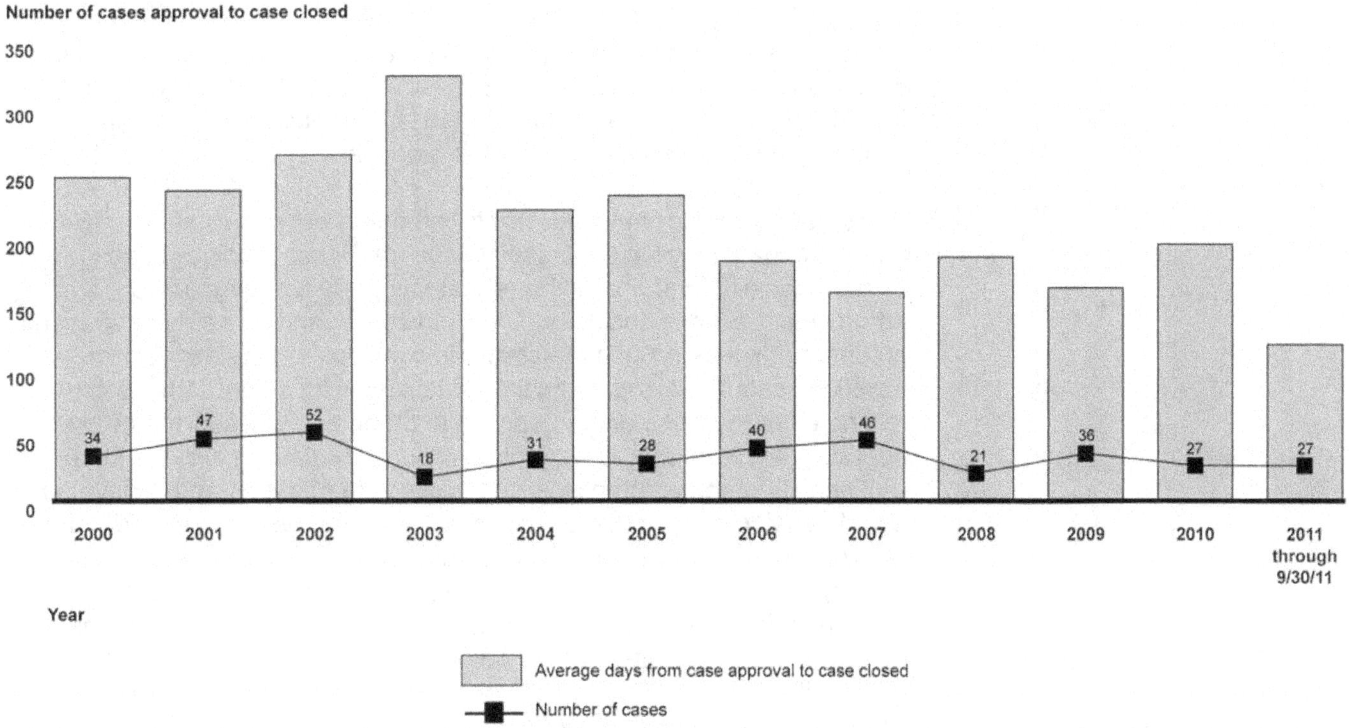

Number of cases approval to case closed

Year

Average days from case approval to case closed

Number of cases

Source: GAO analysis of Interior data.

Policy Changes Intended to Improve Civil Penalty Program Are Under Way

Interior's civil penalty program manager told us that Interior has initiated several efforts to reform the civil penalty program since the *Deepwater Horizon* incident, including addressing human capital issues and responding to recommendations from the September 2010 report of Interior's Outer Continental Shelf Safety Oversight Board.[73]

Human capital. Interior officials reported that, in July 2011, the entire Gulf of Mexico civil penalty program comprised three staff: (1) an experienced civil penalty program manager who has since left the agency; (2) a full-time reviewing officer; and (3) a former Interior official

---

[73]Interior, *Outer Continental Shelf Safety Oversight Board Report to Secretary of the Interior Ken Salazar* (Sept. 1, 2010).

who retired but was rehired on a temporary basis. More recently, in March 2012, Interior hired a new civil penalty program manager and one additional full-time reviewing officer. As Interior increases the number of inspection staff, Interior officials said they anticipate that the number of violations referred for civil penalty review will also increase. According to Interior officials, Interior is attempting to hire additional civil penalty reviewing officers to help manage the workload.

Responding to recommendations. Interior is working to address four recommendations from the Safety Oversight Board report according to Interior officials. First, Interior is reevaluating the full range of its enforcement actions, including fines, violations, and its ability to suspend an operator's lease. Second, Interior is considering whether certain violations should be automatically associated with a fine, rather than relying upon the civil penalty process to determine whether to fine an operator. Third, Interior is working to reduce the time frames for the entire civil penalty process, from referral to collection of a fine, and is developing a civil penalty tracking database, so that management can provide more effective oversight of the process. Fourth, Interior is examining its civil penalty rate structure to determine whether current fine amounts should be adjusted; however, Interior officials stated that any changes to the current civil penalty rate structure would require new legislation or a rulemaking.

Stakeholders Generally Provided Most Substantive Input on Oil and Gas Activities Early in Interior's Lease Sale Planning Process and Reported That Interior's Response Was Mixed

Stakeholders typically provided their most substantive input on Interior's proposed Gulf of Mexico oil and gas activities early in the lease sale planning process and varied in the extent to which they believed Interior considered their concerns. Federal stakeholders said they provided most input while Interior was developing its Gulf of Mexico multilease sale EIS and that Interior was generally responsive to their concerns. State stakeholders indicated that their level of input varied and also said that Interior was generally responsive to their concerns. Nongovernmental industry stakeholder groups stated that Interior has not always been responsive to their concerns and that seemingly inconsistent plan and permit review time frames have made it difficult for companies to plan operations, among other concerns. Nongovernmental conservation stakeholders said that Interior was not always responsive to their concerns. (See app. III for more information on federal and state governmental stakeholders.) Some federal and state stakeholders also told us that opportunities to provide input have recently become more limited because, in 2010, Interior did not renew the charter for a long-standing stakeholder advisory committee.

Federal Stakeholders Provided Input to Interior Early in the Lease Sale Planning Process and Believed Interior Was Generally Responsive to Their Concerns

The federal stakeholders we contacted—officials from NOAA and FWS—said that they generally submitted their most substantive input early in the lease sale planning process when Interior was developing its Gulf of Mexico multilease sale EIS.[74] NOAA and FWS officials told us that historically, they did not review or comment on postlease oil and gas activities, including reviewing exploration and development plans and drilling permits. Various officials at both agencies told us that Interior was generally responsive to their concerns (see app. III for detailed information on stakeholder input).

NOAA

According to NOAA officials, until the *Deepwater Horizon* incident, NOAA provided its most substantive input early in the lease sale planning process, when Interior was developing its Gulf of Mexico multilease sale EIS. Specifically, NEPA regulations direct federal agencies to prepare NEPA analyses, such as EIS documents, concurrently and integrated with other environmental impact analyses to the fullest extent practicable. As such, NOAA's implementation of its responsibilities under the Endangered Species Act, Magnuson-Stevens Fishery Conservation and Management Act, and Marine Mammal Protection Act, generally overlapped with Interior's Gulf of Mexico multilease sale EIS process. NOAA officials explained that, by informally providing input to Interior as it developed its Gulf of Mexico multilease sale EIS,[75] NOAA could ensure that the information necessary to complete its consultations under the Endangered Species Act and the Magnuson-Stevens Fishery Conservation and Management Act were included, as well as any required mitigation measures. As long as these mitigation measures were enforced by Interior, and as long as no new information became available that would require Interior to update the Gulf of Mexico multilease sale EIS, NOAA officials stated that no additional consultations were necessary. As a result, NOAA generally did not request or receive exploration and development plans or drilling permits. (See app. III for more information on NOAA's input into Interior's proposed Gulf of Mexico oil and gas activities from 2002 through January, 2012.)

---

[74]FWS is part of Interior. Therefore, for the purposes of this report, when we state that FWS provided input to Interior, we are stating that FWS provided input to the part of Interior responsible for overseeing offshore oil and gas activities.

[75]In this context, informal means that NOAA did not provide its most substantive input through formally commenting on draft Gulf of Mexico lease sale EISs, rather NOAA staff communicated with Interior staff on an ongoing basis via telephone calls and e-mails to provide input into Interior's Gulf of Mexico lease sale EISs.

NOAA officials told us that Interior has generally been responsive to their input regarding oil and gas development in the Gulf of Mexico, although they have disagreed over how to assess the effects of seismic technologies—frequently used by operators to explore the Gulf of Mexico for oil and gas—on marine mammals. Overall, NOAA officials reported that their primary concerns about oil and gas development in the Gulf of Mexico are the potential effects on marine mammals and fish, including damage to coral reefs, marine debris, vessel strikes of marine life, the risk of an oil spill, and the effects of seismic activities on marine life. Of these issues, assessing the effects from seismic activities on marine mammals has been one of the more challenging issues. Typically, when operators explore for oil and gas in the Gulf of Mexico, they use various seismic technologies that emit powerful sound waves into the water and seafloor to facilitate identifying potential oil and gas resources. According to NOAA officials, the use of these technologies can negatively affect marine mammals, predominantly through behavioral disturbance, but also potentially through hearing impairment or physical injury. NOAA and Interior have been working toward addressing these issues and ensuring environmental compliance for about 10 years.

Since the *Deepwater Horizon* incident, NOAA officials told us that they have reviewed oil spill analyses included in past Gulf of Mexico multilease sale EIS documents. NOAA officials stated that they believe that Interior made a good faith effort to provide accurate scientific data and risk analysis; however, in retrospect, NOAA officials also said that they believe Interior could improve these analyses. For example, NOAA officials told us that it would be difficult to determine the full effect of an oil spill, such as the direction of oil flow and how the oil would affect unique marine life, without better baseline research.[76] At the same time, NOAA officials acknowledged Interior faces financial and technical challenges in obtaining higher quality data.

In addition, on May 19, 2011, Interior and NOAA signed an MOU intended to ensure greater communication and collaboration on oil and gas

---

[76]NOAA officials reported that baseline research, as well as short/long-term monitoring and ocean observing, are important to the oil and gas permitting process in the Gulf of Mexico. At the October 2011 *Deepwater Horizon* Oil Spill Principal Investigator Conference researchers emphasized that there is a lack of baseline information related to living marine resources in the Gulf of Mexico, and that the collection of information is very important to understanding ecosystem processes and oil spill response.

development in the Gulf of Mexico. Specifically, the MOU established a formal agreement regarding the agencies' coordination and collaboration to ensure that decision making related to the development of oil and gas on the OCS is based on relevant scientific information and both agencies' expertise and respective responsibilities and authorities. The MOU specifies that NOAA and Interior will cooperate and coordinate by: (1) defining specific processes to ensure effective and timely communication of agency priorities and upcoming activities; (2) identifying and undertaking critical environmental studies and analyses; (3) collaborating on scientific, environmental, and technical issues related to offshore renewable energy technologies; and (4) increasing coordination and collaboration on public announcements related to OCS activities, including with respect to research and scientific priorities. For example, the MOU created more formal procedures for NOAA's involvement with Interior's OCS energy-related programs and environmental analyses and established quarterly meetings for Interior and NOAA senior leadership to discuss topics relevant to OCS resource development. Under the MOU, NOAA will have a clear role in commenting on both management and science issues and ensuring that both areas receive appropriate attention. When we spoke with a NOAA official about this MOU in July 2011, the official reported that meeting the requirements of the MOU would require additional resources and that NOAA had not yet determined how the specific details of the MOU would be implemented.

FWS

According to FWS officials, FWS also provided its most substantive input early in the lease sale planning process, when Interior was developing its Gulf of Mexico multilease sale EIS. Similar to NOAA, FWS did not typically receive or comment on postlease activities, such as individual exploration and development plans and drilling permits.[77] Again, because NEPA regulations direct federal agencies to prepare EIS documents concurrently and integrated with other environmental impact analyses to the fullest extent practicable, FWS's implementation of its Endangered Species Act responsibilities generally overlap with Interior's Gulf of Mexico multilease sale EIS process. FWS officials explained that by informally providing input to Interior as it develops its Gulf of Mexico multilease sale EIS documents, FWS can ensure that the information

---

[77]According to FWS officials, Interior does request that FWS review each individual lease sale EA covered by the 5-year consultation as they are prepared. The purpose of this review is for Interior to verify that the proposed action has not changed and to ensure that there is no new endangered species information that would need to be addressed.

necessary to complete its consultations under the Endangered Species Act are included, as well as any measures Interior has included to minimize the potential for adverse effects. As long as these measures are enforced by Interior, and no new information becomes available that would require Interior to update the EIS, FWS officials stated that no additional consultations are necessary. As a result, FWS generally did not request or receive exploration and development plans or drilling permits. (See app. III for more information on FWS's input into Interior's proposed Gulf of Mexico oil and gas activities for 2002 through 2012.)[78]

FWS officials reported that Interior has generally been responsive to their concerns regarding proposed oil and gas activities in the Gulf of Mexico since 2002 relating to (1) emergency contingency plans, (2) oil spill risk analyses, and (3) the effects of oil spills on coastal areas.

- *Emergency contingency plans.* FWS officials reported that, during a 2001 consultation related to proposed oil and gas activities from 2003 through 2007, it recommended that Interior continues to require operators to prepare adequate hazardous spill contingency plans for all activities. Further, FWS recommended that such plans include strategic placement of appropriate spill cleanup equipment, personnel training in nonintrusive cleanup technique, and demonstration of response commitment, capabilities, and implementation. Interior, according to FWS officials, has since required all operators to have such a plan.

- *Oil spill risk analyses.* FWS officials told us that they asked to be involved early in the process to model oil spill risk in support of the Gulf of Mexico multilease sale EIS documents. FWS officials stated that, in their 2001 review of the oil spill models that Interior used in its final Gulf of Mexico 2003 to 2007 multilease sale EIS, they raised concerns about assumptions and methodologies that Interior used in preparing the models. FWS requested additional information, which Interior provided, ultimately alleviating many of FWS's concerns.

---

[78]FWS's responsibilities in the OCS under the Endangered Species Act consist primarily of cooperating and assisting other Federal agencies (in this case Interior) to meet their requirements under the act. This is accomplished when another agency presents an action for FWS's review and comment. Depending on the effects to listed species, the end result would be a concurrence letter or biological opinion written by FWS to Interior.

- *Effects of coastal spills.* FWS officials said that they raised concerns about the effect of coastal spills from pipelines and near shore activity associated with the OCS leasing program. According to FWS officials, oil spills can occur along the coastline when pipelines are ruptured, such as in the event a shrimp trawler punctures a pipeline on the seafloor. To respond to this concern, FWS officials told us that Interior must now address the potential effects on the coastal habitats of endangered species from pipelines and other near shore activities associated with the Gulf of Mexico leasing program

Since the *Deepwater Horizon* incident, FWS officials told us that their concerns about oil and gas development in the Gulf of Mexico have evolved. For example, FWS officials said that they believed that deepwater drilling was much more likely to adversely affect species that fall under NOAA's jurisdiction, such as fish and marine mammals. However, the presence of tar balls on beaches along the Gulf Coast after the *Deepwater Horizon* incident, which could negatively affect resources under FWS's jurisdiction, has led FWS to consider taking more precautions when reviewing Interior's Gulf of Mexico multilease sale EIS documents that include proposed deepwater oil and gas development. FWS officials reported telling Interior that they would like more detailed information and validated scientific modeling in Interior's NEPA documents, particularly concerning oil spill risk analysis and cumulative effects of oil and gas activities. Despite the shifts in concerns, FWS told us that they planned no major policy or programmatic changes.

States' Input to Interior Varied, and State Officials Indicated That Interior Was Generally Responsive to Their Concerns

Stakeholders from the five Gulf of Mexico coastal states—Alabama, Florida, Louisiana, Mississippi, and Texas—varied in how they provided input to Interior.[79] Of the five states, two provided comments on Interior's Gulf of Mexico multilease sale EIS documents, according to state officials, and several of the states commented on specific lease sale EIS documents. Officials from all five states reported conducting consistency reviews in accordance with the Coastal Zone Management Act, and one state—twice in the 1990s—found that a proposed oil and gas project in the Gulf of Mexico was inconsistent with its Coastal Zone Management

---

[79]The stakeholders who provided this input were state officials who participated in conducting consistency reviews under the Coastal Zone Management Act, and therefore do not represent the full scope of interaction between Interior and state government officials.

Plan. Officials from all five Gulf of Mexico coastal states told us that Interior has generally been responsive to input they provided about its proposed oil and gas development activities in the Gulf of Mexico, but this responsiveness has varied over time; officials from several states said that they still have concerns associated with oil and gas development in the Gulf of Mexico, including wetland loss, oil spills, and potential effects on both state coastal tourism and deep-sea species and habitats. (See app. III for more information on states' input into Interior's proposed Gulf of Mexico oil and gas activities for 2002 through 2012.)

- *Alabama.* Officials from the Alabama Department of Environmental Management stated they were satisfied with Interior's ability to address their comments even in instances in which they disagreed. Officials explained that both the tourism and fisheries industries are present along the Alabama coast and that they take into consideration any potential effects that oil and gas drilling activities might have on these industries when reviewing Interior's oil and gas NEPA documents. For example, a primary concern to these officials, which was communicated to Interior in 2007, was that they did not want visible structures—such as drilling rigs or production platforms—along the state's coastline.

- *Florida.* Officials from the Florida Department of Environmental Protection characterized Interior as being responsive to their input. Officials explained that their primary concern with oil and gas activities in the Gulf of Mexico was the possibility that an oil spill—whether from a pipeline rupture or well blowout similar to the *Deepwater Horizon* incident—could affect the state's coastal tourism industry. Of the coastal states we reviewed, Florida is unique in that its coastal waters are in Interior's Eastern Planning Area of the Gulf of Mexico, which has had a moratorium on new oil and gas leasing since 1988. However, in 2000, Interior proposed a lease sale that could include areas in the Eastern Planning Area of the Gulf of Mexico. Florida officials, including the Governor, requested that the lease sale be canceled due to long-standing concerns about possible effects on tourism. According to Florida officials, Interior ultimately reduced the size of the area being leased by eliminating areas closest to Florida's coastline.

- *Louisiana.* Officials from Louisiana's Department of Natural Resources' Office of Coastal Management stated that, while historically, they did not find Interior to be responsive to their input, Interior has been more responsive over the past 2 years. Furthermore, these officials stated that relationships with Interior staff, as well as the NEPA and other related documents that they produced, have greatly improved since the *Deepwater Horizon* incident. Officials explained that they are very supportive of OCS leasing and offshore oil and gas development in the Gulf of Mexico but that they still have specific concerns. Officials explained that Louisiana supports the expansion of exploration and development of Gulf energy resources, and all of the nation's natural resources, and believes this is critical to the nation's economic and energy security. However, concerns about how some aspects of OCS leasing are conducted and royalties distributed led Louisiana's Department of Natural Resources to file two lawsuits against Interior in 1991 and again in 2006. The 2006 lawsuit—settled in Louisiana's favor—was filed as a result of Louisiana's long-standing concerns about the techniques used by Interior in its NEPA analyses. State officials told us that Interior had improved, but a report issued by the state in September 2009 identified eight remaining concerns. Specifically, the state was concerned about the adequacy of Interior's analysis of the indirect, secondary, or cumulative effects of lease sales, and that Interior has not verified its predictions of potential environmental and socioeconomic analyses included in its NEPA documents. Louisiana state officials contend that these secondary and cumulative effects cannot be directly attributed to one specific act or event, yet clearly there are secondary and cumulative effects of the development that result from federal lease sales. Louisiana state officials told us that the lease sale stage is the point at which all such potential effects should be addressed because the lease sale is the gateway to any subsequent exploration and development activity within the affected area.

- *Mississippi.* Officials from the Mississippi Department of Marine Resources stated that they were satisfied with Interior's response to their concerns and that they have not had problems cooperating with Interior. Similar to Alabama, officials told us the state's primary concern prior to Hurricane Katrina in 2005 was the drilling of oil and gas wells within 15 miles of the Gulf Island National Seashore's shoreline.

- *Texas.* Officials from the Texas General Land Office stated that, overall, they have had a good working relationship with Interior and that collaboration has been effective. Officials stated that they are primarily concerned about protecting Texas's coastal areas and, in particular, its wetlands, beaches, and oyster reefs. Officials stated that Interior's plans for oil and gas activities have seldom caused concern about possible effects to these areas.

Since the *Deepwater Horizon* incident, officials from all five states told us that no major changes in policies for reviewing Interior's Gulf of Mexico multilease sale EIS and other lease sale EIS documents or conducting consistency reviews have occurred.

Nongovernment Stakeholders Said They Had Few Opportunities to Provide Input and That Interior Was Not Always Responsive to Their Concerns

The nongovernment stakeholders we contacted—representatives from oil and gas industry associations and conservation groups—expressed frustration with the level of input they can provide to Interior and told us that Interior has not always been responsive to their concerns.

Oil and Gas Industry

Representatives from oil and gas industry associations told us that they were satisfied with the process for providing comments on Interior's Gulf of Mexico lease sales, but that since the *Deepwater Horizon* incident, there has been much uncertainty regarding Interior's review and approvals of plans and permits. One representative from an oil and gas association stated that member companies had specified four key issues of concern. First, companies reported inconsistent time frames for reviews of plans and permits, making it difficult for companies to plan operations. Second, companies raised concerns that Interior's staffing was insufficient to review the plans and permits in a timely manner and that Interior staff were uncertain how to comply with new requirements for plans and permits. Third, companies stated that recently issued guidance on new requirements were sometimes contradictory, complicating an operator's efforts to comply with Interior's new policies. Fourth, companies raised concerns that Interior's reliance on notices to lessees and operators amounted to de facto rulemaking outside of the standard regulatory process, which generally results in less opportunity for public comment. Another oil and gas association representative told us that Interior's new policies have been difficult to interpret and that Interior has had to return both exploration and development plans and drilling permit applications to operators for corrections, increasing Interior's review times and delaying approvals. Interior has taken several steps to address this uncertainty, including holding workshops on new policies and making checklists available to provide greater assurance that all required information is submitted with the drilling permit.

Conservation Groups	Representatives of conservation groups we contacted expressed frustration with identifying and accessing operators' exploration and development plans and drilling permits in advance of Interior approvals. Specifically, a conservation group representative told us that the group believed Interior did not routinely make exploration or development plans or drilling permits available to the public for comment prior to approval, and only placed them on its website after being approved. Another representative stated that her conservation group had difficulty locating and commenting on drilling permits and believed that drilling permit information is made available on Interior's website only after drilling approval. Additionally, representatives from conservation groups told us that Interior's website—the principal mechanism to obtain information on proposed oil and gas activities—was difficult to navigate. For example, one representative told us that the website lacked a user friendly mechanism to identify and locate exploration and development plans, stating that it was necessary to know the plan number in order to search for the plan. As a result, conservation group representatives generally expressed dissatisfaction with the amount of information—including exploration and development plans and drilling permits—Interior makes available to the public for oil and gas activities in the Gulf of Mexico.

Representatives from several conservation groups reported that Interior was generally not responsive to concerns they raised about oil and gas activities in the Gulf of Mexico. These representatives reported a range of ongoing concerns, including their view that Interior's management of the Gulf of Mexico has been biased toward development of oil and gas and that there has been a lack of thorough scientific analyses in leasing decisions. Specifically, conservation group representatives said they believed that Interior had relied too heavily on the use of categorical exclusions in approving oil and gas activities as opposed to conducting more thorough, site-specific scientific analyses. A representative from one group stated that either NOAA or another independent scientific agency should have the authority to deny a project when it poses a significant threat to the Gulf of Mexico.

Conservation group representatives also raised concerns that the technology for deepwater drilling may have outpaced oil spill containment and cleanup technologies and the government's capacity to either prevent or address spills when they occur. Compounding that concern was a belief that Interior was too reliant on industries' own assessment of the new containment technologies. Additional concerns these representatives raised included effects to marine mammals from seismic technologies, vessel collisions with marine mammals, and oil spills and other discharges. Because Interior had not addressed their concerns sufficiently, a number of lawsuits have been filed against the Secretary of the Interior for reasons including Interior's use of categorical exclusions for approving oil and gas activities and continued permitting of seismic activities.

Interior Did Not Renew the Charter for a Key Stakeholder Advisory Committee in 2010

In 2010, opportunities for stakeholders to provide input to Interior about offshore leasing activities became more limited because Interior did not renew the charter for a key stakeholder advisory committee—the OCS Policy Committee—that had existed since 1975 and consisted of stakeholders representing federal and state agencies, conservation groups, and industry associations, among others. Under the implementing regulations for the OCS Lands Act, Interior is required to periodically consult with key stakeholders, including state and local governments, oil and gas lessees (operators), and other individuals engaged in OCS activities. Interior's regulations have historically called for consultation between the Secretary of the Interior and OCS stakeholders to take place, in part, through the OCS Policy Committee.[80] The committee's charter called for the committee to review and comment on all aspects of leasing, exploration, development, and protection of OCS resources and states that the committee provides a forum to convey the views representative of coastal states, local governments, offshore industries, environmental communities, other offshore users, and the public. In addition, federal standards for internal control state that federal managers should ensure that there are adequate means of communicating with, and obtaining information that may significantly affect the ability of an agency to achieve its goals from external stakeholders.[81]

In 2010, however, Interior did not renew the committee's charter. Several stakeholders who were former committee participants told us that the committee was an effective mechanism for providing input directly to the Secretary of the Interior and said that they would have liked to have been consulted about actions Interior took after the *Deepwater Horizon* incident. A senior Interior official said that the committee's charter was allowed to lapse because Interior was actively deciding how best to meet the committee's goals, given the increasing complexity of the energy

---

[80]30 C.F.R. §256.19.

[81]GAO/AIMD-00-21.3.1.

industry. The official further explained that the committee's value to Interior has varied over time and that the committee was most successful when it was charged with a specific task, such as examining issues related to the leasing moratorium in the Eastern Planning Area of the Gulf of Mexico. The official stated that reestablishing the committee is an open item for Interior and may be discussed in the future following the reorganization. In the meantime, the official said that industry and environmental groups have other means of providing input to Interior such as meeting directly with Interior officials. Additionally, while Interior no longer has an advisory committee that provides input on leasing on the OCS, the Interior official stated that Interior established a new advisory committee—the Ocean Energy Safety Advisory Committee—to provide input on offshore energy safety. Specifically, this committee is a collaborative initiative among government, industry, academia, and nongovernmental organizations to advise on matters and actions relating to offshore energy safety, including, but not limited to, drilling and workplace safety, well intervention and containment, and oil spill response. Interior officials also stated that they have heard the concerns of stakeholders through frequent workshops, meetings, and public comment periods. They note that Interior's leadership and staff have spent numerous hours devoted to outreach efforts. Interior officials also stated that a Federal Advisory Committee Act (FACA) committee may not always be the most effective manner to receive stakeholder input, and with other outreach measures in place, officials said they do not believe the absence of this committee reflects an internal control compliance issue. Interior has stated that it has an open door policy for all stakeholders, conducting numerous public outreach meetings; stakeholder meetings; public comment periods; meetings with industry, state and local officials, and nongovernment organizations; and workshops and conferences.

Following Interior's Reorganization, Key Challenges Remain

Since its reorganization, Interior faces six key challenges in its oversight of offshore oil and gas activities in the Gulf of Mexico. These challenges include Interior's ability to: (1) prospectively categorize drilling operations according to risk; (2) implement effective IT systems; (3) hire, retain, and train qualified staff; (4) respond to recommendations from external reviews; (5) develop and implement timely and effective regulations; and (6) adapt to constrained resources.

Interior Has Taken Steps to Identify and Evaluate Drilling Risks, but Its Capacity to Do So Remains Limited

Since the *Deepwater Horizon* incident, Interior has taken steps to identify and evaluate drilling risks, but its capacity to do so remains limited. Federal standards for internal control state that agency management should identify relevant risks from internal and external sources and analyze their potential effects.[82] Such an analysis generally includes estimating the risk's significance, assessing the likelihood of its occurrence, and deciding how to manage the risk and what actions should be taken. Interior officials stated that they have the technical capacity to prospectively categorize proposed drilling operations according to risk but they have not done so, though they acknowledged such an effort could improve Interior's oversight of offshore oil and gas activities. Prospectively categorizing risk helps ensure that oversight resources are effectively allocated.

Interior officials told us they can devote additional resources to certain drilling operations that they believe may be challenging. For example, Interior officials told us that district engineers are aware that drilling certain wells is likely to pose greater risks, such as drilling exploratory wells and wells at depths greater than 15,000 feet, and may require a more rigorous review. More recently, since the *Deepwater Horizon* incident, Interior officials told us that Interior, in a joint effort with industry, developed a well containment screening tool to assess well design, the geology surrounding the well site, reservoir pressures, and wellbore fluid gradient requirements. According to these officials, the screening tool is primarily intended to assess whether a well may be contained following a subsea well blowout, but that they also use the screening tool to evaluate overall well design based on risk.

Interior officials told us that once drilling is under way, district engineers receive from operators weekly well activity reports, which they review to ensure compliance with the specifications contained in the drilling permit. Each weekly well activity report also includes a checklist of 12 "significant events," including such items as rig failure, well kick occurrence, and stuck drilling pipe.[83] Interior officials told us that systematically analyzing

---

[82]GAO/AIMD-00-21.3.1.

[83]A well kick is an entry of water, gas, oil, or other formation fluid into the wellbore during drilling. It occurs when the pressure exerted by the column of drilling fluid is not great enough to overcome the pressure exerted by the fluids in the formation drilled. If prompt action is not taken to control the kick, or kill the well, a blowout may occur. A stuck pipe is when a drill pipe has inadvertently become immovable in the wellbore.

these reports could provide information on drilling risk. For example, based on the information in these reports, Interior may be able to improve its data on what geographic areas, specific drilling rigs, or operators are associated with higher risks for drilling operations, which could allow them to better prospectively categorize drilling risks. However, Interior officials told us they have not had the resources to systematically analyze data reported in the weekly well activity reports. In addition, Interior has not specifically defined all "significant events." As a result, even if Interior had the resources to analyze its weekly well activity reports, it may find that the information they contain on the 12 significant events is inconsistent because the agency does not have clear definitions for some of these significant events.

Interior officials also told us that district engineers who have concerns about a particular well may request additional inspections of certain drilling operations, although when such requests are made, Interior does not track them in its TIMS IT system. Additionally, Interior has a documented policy to more frequently inspect operators that have poor performance records. Specifically, Interior generates a monthly operator compliance report that includes operators and specific facilities that require special on-site inspections or attention based on their compliance history. Interior's district offices can include an operator on this report based on several criteria, including violations that resulted in a serious injury or fatality and violations forwarded for civil penalty reviews. Once an operator or facility is included in this report, Interior's policy is to inspect its operations at least once every 4 months, using a combination of announced and unannounced inspections, among other actions. Interior removes the operator or facility from the report when it determines that the operator's performance and compliance history improves. However, an Interior official told us that Interior did not begin to systematically track which operators were included on the compliance report and their associated inspection in its TIMS IT system until 2011. Accordingly, we were unable to verify the extent to which operators were included on the monthly operator compliance report and whether those operators were inspected according to Interior's policy. Overall, Interior remains unable to demonstrate how it deploys its inspection resources in such a manner that takes into account a prospective categorization of drilling according to risk, whether the risk is technical—such as drilling into high pressure, high temperature reservoirs—or associated with operators or facilities with a history of poor compliance.

Some entities have expressed concern that Interior does not have a policy to categorize proposed drilling operations based on risk. In January

2011, the report of the National Commission on the BP Deepwater Horizon Oil Spill and Offshore Drilling recommended that Interior, with the help of the National Academy of Engineering, cultivate and maintain expertise on offshore drilling safety by identifying criteria and establishing a methodology for assessing high-risk wells in collaboration with the U.S. Geological Survey, the Department of Energy, NOAA, and academia, and developing the capability to perform sophisticated risk assessments.[84] Interior officials told us that, while they have taken some actions related to the recommendation, they have not specifically followed through with the recommendation, and an official from the National Academy of Engineering told us that it was unaware of any ongoing discussions between Interior and the National Academy of Engineering on this issue.

Interior officials stated that a potential project that industry may sponsor would, among other things, quantitatively assign a risk score to proposed wells based on factors such as well location, well design, and other technical considerations. Interior officials stated that they would like to participate in this project, although they recognize Interior would have to contribute to the project financially. If successful, the project could result in a tool that Interior could require operators to use as part of its permit review process. Interior officials explained that there is a precedent for this type of collaboration; after Hurricanes Katrina and Rita, they worked with industry to develop an analytical tool to identify the risk of structures breaking free from their mooring. Operators may now include the results of this tool with their drilling permit applications. However, without a more systematic and prospective approach to identifying and categorizing drilling risk, Interior may not effectively devote its limited oversight resources—including engineering reviews of drilling permits, monitoring weekly well activity reports, and inspecting drilling operations—in a manner that most effectively mitigates risk.

---

[84]National Commission, *Deep Water: The Gulf Oil Disaster and the Future of Offshore Drilling*, Report to the President (January 2011).

Interior Continues to Face Challenges Implementing Effective IT Systems

As we reported in September 2007,[85] Interior has faced challenges implementing effective IT systems, which has affected its ability to meet program and mission goals in overseeing oil and gas development in the OCS. We found that these challenges persist. In particular, we found two challenges with Interior's current IT systems.

First, Interior initiated a major IT project in 2003 called OCS Connect that did not meet user needs or planned delivery dates. At that time, Interior reported that its offshore leasing program relied heavily on paper-based processes and that technology improvements would allow it to streamline its business processes.[86] OCS Connect was designed to replace some of Interior's existing IT systems—including its TIMS IT system—and improve and expand stakeholders' access to information, decrease Interior's processing time for reviews of plans and drilling permits, and increase the quality and quantity of the analyses of offshore resources, among other things. Additionally, a key goal of OCS Connect was that it would allow Interior to track the life cycle of a specific oil and gas development from initial leasing, through planning, permitting, and compliance. OCS Connect was initially designed to include 14 processes—called business process clusters—that Interior had identified as potential candidates for reengineering, such as managing drilling plan submittals and permit requests. A senior Interior official said that Interior hired a contractor to gather system requirements from agency staff and develop OCS Connect. The contractor developed the first of the 14 clusters, but it was poorly received by Interior staff and did not meet their needs. Subsequent problems, including Hurricane Katrina in 2005, led to delays in developing the remaining clusters. In July 2008, we reported that the Office of Management and Budget identified OCS Connect as a high-risk project that was poorly planned.[87] On December 31, 2010, after obligating approximately $67 million toward the development of OCS Connect, according to an Interior official estimate, and following several

---

[85]GAO, *Information Technology: Further Improvements Needed to Identify and Oversee Poorly Planned and Performing Projects*, GAO-07-1211T (Washington, D.C.: Sept. 20, 2007).

[86]Outer Continental Shelf (OCS) Connect Initiative (Request for Comments concerning Offshore Minerals Management Program's e-Government Initiative)." 68 *Fed. Reg.* 46656 (2003).

[87]GAO, *Information Technology: OMB and Agencies Need to Improve Planning, Management, and Oversight of Projects Totaling Billions of Dollars*, GAO-08-1051T (Washington, D.C.: July 31, 2008).

changes to its scope, Interior officially terminated the project, citing the ongoing reorganization of BOEM and BSEE. Interior officials and agency documentation reported that 1 of the 14 clusters was complete, development had begun on some others, and some software and hardware had been upgraded. A senior Interior official said that Interior learned a number of lessons from this experience, many of which were formally documented. One of the key lessons learned was that the contractor limited the amount of feedback end users could provide throughout the development process, which contributed to the problems with the project. As a result, Interior's offshore leasing program continues without the technology improvements that would allow it to streamline its business processes. Because Interior has yet to fully replace or upgrade the IT systems used for overseeing offshore oil and gas developments, it continues to have problems with its GIS used to facilitate NEPA analyses and the TIMS IT system used to track operators' exploration and development plans and records with more accurate and efficient systems. As noted previously, officials in the Gulf of Mexico regional office told us that GIS is hindered by the poor quality of data in the system. Furthermore, Interior's TIMS IT system lacks edit checks to limit operators' ability to submit incomplete or inaccurate plans, making Interior's review of exploration and development plans challenging. In addition, the method by which amendments are currently tracked in the TIMS IT system can complicate and lengthen Interior's review process. As of September 2011, Interior staff were working with the consultant that facilitated the reorganization to create a requirements document for ePlans, which is designed to address the shortcomings in the TIMS IT system. However, some Interior officials expressed concern that Interior's experience going forward with ePlans could be similar to its experience with OCS Connect.[88]

Second, BOEM and BSEE do not have a current comprehensive IT strategic plan. Interior's most recent IT strategic plan is dated 2005 to 2007 and was developed for MMS. Senior Interior officials said that they have not updated the IT strategic plan because they were focused on the reorganization and were addressing only those IT issues related to the reorganization, such as the division of IT support resources. The officials said that they anticipated developing a plan within the next few months,

---

[88]In addition, as previously discussed in this report, Interior also has not fully implemented a 2009 pilot program that would allow inspection staff to electronically access and review operators' records while onshore.

but were currently in the very early stages of the process. In January 2004, we identified well-defined IT strategic planning as an important component of effective management because it helps ensure that an agency's IT goals are aligned with its strategic goals and that IT is being used to maximize improvement in mission performance.[89] Additionally, in 2009, we reported that IT strategic plans should serve as the agency's IT vision or road map and help align its information resources with its business strategies and investment decisions.[90] Further, an IT strategic plan comprising results-orientated goals, strategies, milestones, and performance measures is important to enable an agency to consider the resources, including human capital, infrastructure, and funding, that are needed to implement, manage, support, and pay for IT projects. For example, a strategic plan that identifies what an agency intends to accomplish during a given period helps ensure that the necessary infrastructure is put in place for new or improved IT capabilities. In addition, a strategic plan that identifies interdependencies within and across individual IT systems modernization projects helps ensure that the interdependencies are understood and managed, so that projects—and thus system solutions—are effectively integrated. Without an effective IT strategic plan, Interior will find it more difficult to address the challenges it faces in implementing effective IT systems, potentially limiting its abilities to meet programmatic and system modernization goals.

Interior Continues to Report Challenges in Hiring, Retaining, and Training Staff as Well As Succession Planning

We have previously reported that Interior has faced persistent challenges in hiring and retaining qualified staff in key oil and gas engineering and inspection positions. In particular, in March 2010, we reported that Interior lacked staff with critical skills because of difficulties in hiring, training, and retaining staff.[91] In February 2011, when we added Interior's management of oil and gas resources to our list of areas at high risk for waste, fraud, abuse, and mismanagement or in need of broad reform,[92] we cited human capital challenges as a key concern. We found during this review that

---

[89]GAO, *Information Technology Management: Governmentwide Strategic Planning, Performance Measurement, and Investment Management Can Be Further Improved,* GAO-04-49 (Washington, D.C.: Jan. 12, 2004).

[90]GAO, *Information Technology: FDA Needs to Establish Key Plans and Processes for Guiding Systems Modernization Efforts,* GAO-09-523 (Washington, D.C.: June 2, 2009).

[91]GAO-10-313.

[92]GAO-11-278.

human capital problems persist as Interior undergoes its reorganization, which increases the need for key positions such as engineers and inspectors. In addition, Interior has not developed a comprehensive strategic workforce plan that outlines specific strategies to address gaps in critical skills and competencies that need attention and processes to address human capital challenges, including determining the critical skills and competencies that will be needed to achieve current and future programmatic results, and help guide future human capital management.

Challenges in Hiring Staff

A senior Interior official told us that hiring qualified engineers and inspectors poses the greatest human capital challenge. In particular, the official told us that hiring qualified engineers is difficult because the federal salary schedule sets starting salaries for entry-level engineers at Interior at about $30,000 to $40,000 less per year than an entry-level position in the private sector—a difference of about 50 percent. The $30,000 to $40,000 gap between the federal and private sector salaries persists throughout engineers' careers, although as an Interior engineer's salary rises over time, it decreases as a percentage of total salary. Locality pay differentials within the federal salary schedule also mean that workers in Louisiana are paid less than those in Houston, TX; therefore, Interior's Gulf of Mexico offices are competing with both government and private-sector employers located in Houston that can pay higher salaries. Interior regional office officials also noted that the current federal pay freeze, which eliminates cost-of-living adjustments for federal employees, may further deter inspectors from seeking or continuing employment with Interior. Regional office officials also stated that because the private sector offers higher starting salaries than the federal government, top candidates are typically hired by the petroleum industry, with Interior attracting less skilled candidates. To address pay challenges, in December of 2011, Congress provided a special 25 percent base pay increase for geologists, geophysicists, and petroleum engineers in the Gulf of Mexico region.[93] Further, in February 2012, Interior announced expanded student loan repayment for engineers and certain technical staff. In addition to pay, Interior officials stated that the small number of petroleum engineering programs in the United States, as well as constraints on hiring non-U.S. citizens for federal positions, means that the pool of qualified candidates is limited. To attract applicants, a senior Interior official said that recruiting has begun to focus on midlevel career

---

[93]Pub. L. No. 112-74, div. E, title I, § 121(c), 125 Stat. 1012 (2011).

engineers in the private sector who may be interested in working for Interior because the agency offers a more standard work week and family-friendly work environment than the private sector, including working most days onshore versus months away from home and overseas. For inspectors, a senior Interior official stated that, similar to engineers, the primary challenge is recruiting highly qualified candidates. This official also stated that, unlike the situation for engineers, the pay difference between Interior inspectors and comparable positions in the private sector is not as great, but stricter federal hiring standards disqualify many potential applicants. For example, conflicts of interest could disqualify candidates from federal jobs but may not limit their prospects in the private sector.

Challenges in Retaining Staff

A senior Interior official stated that retaining qualified engineers was less of an issue than recruitment. Interior engineers tend to spend less time offshore on drilling rigs and production platforms than those in the private sector, meaning that they have more time with their families. Government work is also typically less cyclical than that in the private sector, providing more job security. The senior Interior official stated that the better work-life balance and relative job security meant that the engineers they are able to recruit typically stay. Nonetheless, regional office officials expressed some concern about retention and recent attrition. Specifically, one regional office official noted that the Gulf of Mexico regional office had recently lost four of its five experienced engineers.

Interior's headquarters and Gulf of Mexico regional office officials also noted that retention of inspectors has been a challenge in the aftermath of the *Deepwater Horizon* incident. Many senior staff left the agency, and new requirements that Interior implemented in response to the oil spill have led to an increase in work demands without a commensurate increase in compensation, which may increase attrition. Specifically, several officials from the Gulf of Mexico regional office noted that new requirements for witnessing blowout preventer tests significantly increased the number of days inspectors must spend offshore. As with engineers, regional office officials said that one of the key advantages that Interior offers over positions in the private sector is that its inspectors can generally be home each night; therefore increased time offshore might cause inspectors to migrate to better-paying jobs in the private sector. In June 2011, a senior Interior official stated that Interior received a strong response from its inspector job announcements in the Gulf of Mexico and hired 30 new inspectors; however, attrition limited the net gain to 15 inspectors. As of March 2012, Interior was able to hire an additional 13 inspectors while losing 9, resulting in a total net gain of 19 inspectors since the *Deepwater Horizon* incident.

Retirements were cited as a significant issue by Interior officials, as many senior staff are now eligible or will soon be eligible for retirement. According to data provided by Interior, as of January 2012, approximately 45 percent of BOEM and 42 percent of BSEE staff will be eligible for retirement over the next 5 years. Regional office officials were particularly concerned about the loss of senior staff following the reorganization, noting that until they can refine and document many new processes, they depend on the expertise of their senior staff to fulfill their missions. Interior's human capital planning documents, as well as officials in both headquarters and the Gulf of Mexico regional office, noted that long-term succession planning was a major issue and that, in many cases, positions were "one deep"—meaning that if experienced staff left the agency, there would not be enough skilled staff to take their place.

Challenges in Training Staff

In June 2011, in response to concerns with developing newer staff, Interior announced the opening of a new National Offshore Training and Learning Center and the development of the agency's first formal training curriculum for inspectors and engineers. An official responsible for overseeing inspectors and engineers stated that the development of the training program may be one of the most important accomplishments to come out of the reorganization. Interior officials told us that, historically, Interior has not had a formal inspector training program; rather, it relied on on-the-job training that included pairing senior inspectors with newly hired inspectors and some classroom instruction. Senior and regional office officials stated that this type of training produced inconsistent results, as some senior inspectors proved to be less effective trainers than others. Additionally, following the *Deepwater Horizon* incident, Interior's Office of Inspector General reported that, based on survey results, only 39 percent of inspectors believed that they had received sufficient training to perform their duties effectively. The training center's director stated that the center will eventually provide training for inspectors, engineers, and environmental enforcement officers, although the first priority is to establish a core curriculum to train inspection staff. The director stated that the inspection staff training curriculum would eventually consist of 25 modules covering a range of issues. As of December 2011, 1 module had been developed and was being revised by the new training director. Overall, the director stated that the inspection training curriculum will include classroom training, testing, on-the-job training, and potentially some form of certification. Additionally, as part of the inspection training curriculum, the director plans to incorporate various simulators, thereby allowing inspectors to experience real-world situations. For example, according to the director, Interior plans to use a fully operational drilling platform simulator operated by Louisiana State University, as well as a working production platform to allow inspectors to train in a more realistic environment. In December 2011, the director stated that training for engineers will eventually be developed but that because engineers generally have well-developed technical skills, the curriculum will focus on problem solving rather than obtaining and developing specific technical skills. More recently, in March 2012, Interior officials stated that it had initiated technical training for engineers. Interior officials stated that they have adjusted the training program to provide training for both engineers and inspectors in the first year of employment, use a comprehensive training plan to address the needs of the current and expanding workforce, and added an enhanced technical curriculum. While we note Interior's action to date, Interior has not yet finalized its training modules, and no inspection staff have been certified. Until Interior has successfully developed, finalized, and implemented a training program for inspectors and engineers, Interior will find it more difficult to provide adequate oversight of offshore oil and gas activities in the Gulf.

Absence of Comprehensive Strategic Workforce Planning

Interior is taking steps to respond to its human capital challenges, but it has not developed a comprehensive strategic workforce plan that outlines specific strategies and processes to help address these challenges and help guide future human capital management for BOEM and BSEE. In January 2001, we determined that strategic human capital management merited designation as a governmentwide high-risk area because the government's approach to managing its people—its human capital—was the critical missing link in reforming and modernizing the federal government's management practices.[94] In a December 2003 report, we identified strategic human capital, or workforce, planning as the key to addressing two critical organizational needs: (1) aligning an organization's human capital program with its current and emerging mission and programmatic goals and (2) developing long-term strategies for acquiring, developing, and retaining staff to achieve programmatic goals.[95] In that report, we identified five key principles that effective human capital planning should address. For example, effective workforce planning

---

[94]GAO, *High-Risk Series: An Update*, GAO-01-263 (Washington, D.C.: January 2001).

[95]GAO, *Human Capital: Key Principles for Effective Strategic Workforce Planning*, GAO-04-39 (Washington, D.C.: Dec. 11, 2003).

should determine the critical skills and competencies that will be needed to achieve current and future programmatic results and develop strategies to address gaps and human capital conditions in critical skills and competencies that need attention, such as for succession planning and addressing short-term human capital needs for critical skills. Prior to the reorganization, Interior developed a strategic workforce plan for MMS for 2008 through 2013 and a similar workforce plan for MMS's Gulf of Mexico region in March of 2010, but it has not adapted these plans to the new organizational structure. Following the *Deepwater Horizon* incident, Interior took steps to improve its human capital planning in response to recommendations from external reviews and as part of the reorganization. For example, in response to a recommendation from Interior's Office of Inspector General, Interior developed a succession plan for its regional offices. Most recently, in March 2012 Interior issued a departmentwide strategic workforce management plan and indicated that it would implement more detailed workforce planning. However, without a strategic workforce plan for both BOEM and BSEE, Interior may find it more challenging to address human capital challenges such as hiring, retention, and training. Senior Interior officials said that they would eventually develop a plan for BOEM and BSEE, but that they did not have the time or the resources to do so because of the demands placed upon them by the reorganization. To date, Interior has not specifically identified when it plans to develop such a plan.

While improved workforce planning will assist Interior in meeting BOEM and BSEE's agency-wide goals, both agencies will still likely face significant human capital challenges in coming years. For example, a 2011 study by Schlumberger Business Consulting,[96] an oil and gas services company, reported that the oil and gas industry is going through a major transition referred to as the "big crew change," as many workers hired before significant recruitment cuts in the 1980s are now approaching retirement. The report projected a significant net loss in experienced petroleum technicians by 2015 due to retirements and concluded that while recruitment should compensate for the total number of employees lost, a significant experience gap will remain, threatening the timely completion of projects.

---

[96]Schlumberger Business Consulting, 2011 SBC Oil & Gas HR Benchmark, March 8, 2012.

Interior Has Not Consistently Tracked Recommendations from External Reviews

Interior had not consistently tracked recommendations from external reviews examining Interior's oversight of oil and gas activities issued after the *Deepwater Horizon* incident until March 2012, when it provided documentation that it had begun developing a database to consistently track recommendations. Under federal standards for internal control,[97] agencies are to ensure that the findings of audits and other reviews are promptly resolved under the monitoring standard. Specifically, agency managers should (1) promptly evaluate findings from audits and other reviews, including those showing deficiencies and recommendations reported by auditors and others who evaluate agency operations; (2) determine proper actions in response to findings and recommendations from those audits and reviews; and (3) complete, within established time frames, all actions that correct or otherwise resolve the matters brought to management's attention.[98] Following the *Deepwater Horizon* incident, various federal entities reported on factors that contributed to the *Deepwater Horizon* incident and made a number of recommendations to Interior to improve its oversight of oil and gas drilling operations and help prevent such incidents. Federal government reviews on the *Deepwater Horizon* incident include the following:

- The postaccident safety report that the President directed Interior to prepare within 30 days of the accident, issued on May 27, 2010;[99]

- A review of Interior's NEPA policies, practices, and procedures by the President's Council on Environmental Quality, issued on August 16, 2010;[100]

---

[97]GAO/AIMD-00-21.3.1.

[98]The resolution process begins when audit or other review results are reported to management and is completed only after action has been taken that (1) corrects identified deficiencies, (2) produces improvements, or (3) demonstrates the findings and recommendations do not warrant management action.

[99]U.S. Department of the Interior, *Increased Safety Measures for Energy Development on the Outer Continental Shelf* (May 27, 2010).

[100]Council on Environmental Quality. August 16, 2010.

- A report by the OCS Safety Oversight Board—a group established by the Interior's Secretary following the *Deepwater Horizon* incident—issued on September 1, 2010;[101]

- A report by Interior's Office of Inspector General issued on December 7, 2010;[102]

- A report by the National Commission on the BP Deepwater Horizon Oil Spill and Offshore Drilling issued on January 11, 2011;[103]

- A joint accident investigation report by Interior and the U.S. Coast Guard issued on September 14, 2011;[104,105] and

- A report by the National Academy of Engineering on December 14, 2011.[106]

We found that Interior is formally tracking recommendations from several reports, including those issued by Interior's Office of Inspector General and the OCS Safety Oversight Board. According to Interior's Office of Inspector General, as of March 2012, Interior has implemented 29 of the 64 recommendations included in its December 2010 report.[107]

---

[101]U.S. Department of the Interior. September 1, 2010.

[102]U.S. Department of the Interior Office of Inspector General, *A New Horizon: Looking to the Future of the Bureau of Ocean Energy Management, Regulation, and Enforcement*, CR-EV-MMS-0015-2010 (Dec. 7, 2010).

[103]National Commission, *Deep Water: The Gulf Oil Disaster and the Future of Offshore Drilling*, Report to the President (January 2011).

[104]The Bureau of Ocean Energy Management Regulation and Enforcement, *Report Regarding the Causes of the April 20, 2010, Macondo Well Blowout* (Sept. 14, 2011).

[105]United States Coast Guard: *Report of Investigation into the Circumstances Surrounding the Explosion, Fire, Sinking and Loss of Eleven Crew Members Aboard the Mobile Offshore Drilling Unit* Deepwater Horizon. In the Gulf of Mexico, April 20-22, 2010. Volume I of the report was released on April 20, 2011.

[106]National Academy of Engineering and National Research Council, *Macondo Well-Deepwater Horizon Blowout* (Dec. 14, 2011).

[107]Oil and Gas and Sulfur Operations in the Outer Continental Shelf—Increased Safety Measures for Energy Development on the Outer Continental Shelf, 75 *Fed. Reg.* 63346 (2010).

However, Interior has not consistently employed a process for tracking and responding to the findings and recommendations of other external reviews. The national commission's report on the BP Oil Spill[108] made recommendations covering 31 areas. In September 2011, we asked a senior Interior official about the national commission's recommendations and the agency's response. Interior was able to provide responses on specific recommendations but was unable to provide documentation that tracked the steps Interior had taken to address the national commission's recommendations. According to the official, the national commission's report was directed to the President; therefore, Interior was not required or expected to officially document its response to the report's recommendations. Moreover, according to the official, Interior's reorganization, along with other policy changes enacted since the *Deepwater Horizon* incident, has likely addressed the recommendations in the national commission's report. However, in March 2012, Interior provided documentation tracking the national commission's recommendations and announced on March 14, 2012, that several members of the national commission were forming a new organization— the Oil Spill Commission Action— to monitor the progress of government and industry to implement a series of critical safety recommendations outlined in its January 2011 report. On April 17, 2012, the Oil Spill Commission Action released a progress report stating that while it was encouraged by the advances industry, Interior, and other federal agencies had made in the 2 years since the *Deepwater Horizon* incident to improve the safety of offshore drilling and the nation's readiness to respond to any spills that do occur, it noted that more needs to be done, including by Congress, which has yet to enact any legislation responding to the explosion and spill. Furthermore, Interior's BSEE indicated that it had recently developed a database to track recommendations from all recently issued reports and planned to systematically enter and track recommendations from all relevant reports. Nonetheless, Interior has not consistently employed a formal process for tracking and responding to the findings and recommendations of external reviews and ensured they are promptly resolved. Without taking steps to document that such findings and recommendations are resolved by correcting identified deficiencies, producing improvements, or demonstrating that the findings and recommendations do not warrant

[108]National Commission, *Deep Water: The Gulf Oil Disaster and the Future of Offshore Drilling*, Report to the President (January 2011).

management action, Interior cannot, for example, demonstrate to decision makers and reviewers that it considered the national commission's recommendations for improving oversight and what actions, if any, Interior has taken to implement them.

Interior Continues to Face Challenges Issuing Effective and Timely Regulations for Deepwater Drilling Activities

Interior officials stated that the rate of technology development in deepwater drilling has surpassed Interior's ability to draft and publish regulations and that, even prior to the *Deepwater Horizon* incident, Interior was already taking a stopgap approach to provide regulatory oversight. Specifically, instead of updating regulations to address new technologies and processes, Interior has to some extent, relied on Notices to Lessees and Operators to communicate new policies and regulatory approaches. Additionally in 2005, Interior began requiring operators to submit a Deepwater Operations Plan for deepwater projects.[109] According to Interior officials, the Deepwater Operations Plan is designed to address industry and Interior concerns by notifying an operator in advance of significant investment whether Interior accepted the operator's plan. According to an Interior official, because Interior does not have any regulations specific to deepwater environments, the Deepwater Operations Plan functioned in lieu of regulations. However, without up-to-date regulations on current technologies and practices, the incidence of requests for departures from existing regulations is likely to increase.

Interior officials stated that many activities on deepwater operations in the Gulf of Mexico are not covered by existing regulations and that, therefore, operators' departure requests are common. Departure requests potentially increase the risks associated with certain drilling operations because district engineers are making decisions independently and often without documented guidance, which can result in regulations being inconsistently applied. For example, the OCS Safety Oversight Board's report found that operators will "shop around" district offices for approval for departure requests. We attempted to analyze Interior's data from

---

[109]30 C.F.R. §§ 250.286–295; see also NTL No. 2011-N11 issued Nov. 21, 2011. Prior to issuing new regulations, Interior began requiring certain information from operators working in water depths greater than 1,000 feet through the establishment of handling procedures for Deepwater Operation Plans in 1997. In October 2000, Interior issued NTL No. 2000-N06, which provided guidance on Deepwater Operations Plan submission requirements.

Interior's TIMS IT system on departure requests but found that the data were incomplete and unreliable. Specifically, Interior officials reported that they did not record departure request denials. When we analyzed approved departure requests—which Interior guidance states district engineers should record—Interior officials reported that engineers were no longer recording that information consistently in the TIMS IT system. However, officials stated that accurate data on departure requests, approvals, and denials, would help Interior identify specific regulations that should be considered for revision.

In response to the *Deepwater Horizon* incident, as noted previously, Interior issued a number of new policies affecting offshore oil and gas operations and is taking steps to improve its ability to develop and issue final regulations; however, Interior continues to face challenges issuing effective and timely regulations. An Interior official stated that, following the *Deepwater Horizon* incident, there was a significant shift to focus on ensuring that Interior has effective regulations. Additionally, according to an Interior official, Interior's senior management have taken a more active role in discussions regarding regulations than have directors of the predecessor agency, MMS. An Interior official stated that the new requirements—including regulations—issued in the period following the *Deepwater Horizon* incident are not typical of the agencies' processes and that they were issued much more quickly than typical regulations. Interior documents acknowledge a historic weakness in the agency not issuing timely and effective regulations.

Representatives of API, which publishes standards for oil and gas activities frequently incorporated into Interior's regulations, stated that although API fully supported an effective regulatory regime, it was concerned about the effectiveness of Interior's rulemaking, especially rulemaking in response to the *Deepwater Horizon* incident. API representatives stated that the interim final drilling safety rule Interior issued in October 2010 created burdens for operators and potentially undermined the effectiveness of some existing regulations.[110] Specifically, API publishes standards generally agreed upon by industry and regulators, and where applicable, Interior incorporated some of these standards into its regulations. These standards typically state that an operator "should" or "shall" follow some specified practice or procedure;

---

[110]75 *Fed. Reg.* 63346 (2010).

however, an API representative stated that the interim final drilling safety rule, which applies to many API standards referenced by Interior's regulations, requires that operators "must" follow the specified practice or procedure. In some circumstances, according to an API representative, this revision undermined the standards' effectiveness, may increase risk, and created substantial new requirements for operators. In a letter to the Regulations and Standards Branch of BOEMRE on December 13, 2010, trade and industry groups stated that revising a section on well control and blowout preventer maintenance to include mandatory requirements would increase the risk to worker safety due to increased blowout preventer handling requirements.[111]

In addition to concerns raised specifically by API, industry representatives also stated that, by relying so heavily on Notices to Lessees and Operators, Interior is not following the formal rulemaking process, limiting the public's—including industry's—opportunities for involvement and undermining the transparency of the process. Despite concerns regarding Interior's rulemaking, API representatives noted that Interior has recently become more involved in API's standard-setting meetings since the *Deepwater Horizon* incident. In particular, representatives stated that Interior staff regularly attended meetings and provided formal comments on new standards that API is developing for deepwater well design.[112] Additionally, API officials stated that they worked with industry to provide recommendations in May 2010 for Interior to consider in its review of its regulatory scheme. Later, in September 2010, industry provided recommendations to both Interior and the Coast Guard on well intervention and oil spill response.

Interior has taken steps to reexamine and improve the processes used to develop regulations since the *Deepwater Horizon* incident. For example, Interior is working with industry to improve regulations specific to deepwater drilling and hosted a conference in November 2011 to discuss these efforts. In addition, Interior officials stated that they had recently contracted with Argonne National Laboratory to review BSEE's current

---

[111]API, the International Association of Drilling Contractors, the Independent Petroleum Association of America, the National Ocean Industries Association, the Offshore Operators Committee, the Offshore Equipment and Operating Procedures Joint Industry Task Forces, and the US Oil and Gas Association submitted comments.

[112]API Recommended Practice 96, Deepwater Well Design and Construction, 1st Ed. 201X.

regulations and make recommendations on how it can improve those regulations.

While Interior has taken steps to issue new regulations and improve its regulatory processes following the *Deepwater Horizon* incident, it will also continue to face challenges in this area in coming years. In particular, Interior staff noted that industry is drilling more wells into reservoirs associated with high temperatures and pressures. These drilling operations can be more challenging than other operations. For example, in late March 2012, a high pressure and high temperature well in the North Sea began leaking gas, causing the evacuation of the platform due to the potential risk of an explosion and fire. In May 2012, the platform's operator announced that the leak had been stopped.

Interior Anticipates That Resource Constraints Could Limit Efforts to Increase Its Oversight Capacity

Interior officials told us that Interior had planned to increase its oversight capacity—including hiring additional staff and improving support service— through a multiyear expansion plan, with full staffing anticipated in fiscal year 2013. As of September 2011, Interior officials expressed concern that current and potential future budgetary constraints may prevent Interior from increasing its capacity as anticipated. In particular, Gulf of Mexico regional office officials expressed concerns that they may not receive the anticipated increases in resources for staffing and helicopter operating costs, which would hinder their ability to review permits and conduct inspections. Without the resources initially anticipated, officials said that they will not be able to fully develop their programs as planned, potentially hindering their ability to manage oil and gas activities in the Gulf of Mexico. However, in March 2012, officials told us that the fiscal year 2012 appropriations bill included an inspection fee of $62 million, allowing BSEE to receive most of the resources needed to increase its inspection and permitting capacity. Despite these new fees, Interior officials expressed concern that attention to oversight of offshore oil and gas drilling may diminish over time and that future budget appropriations may be limited, hindering their ability to provide effective oversight.

Conclusions

The Department of the Interior is charged with the critical role of ensuring that the country's oil and gas resources on the OCS in the Gulf of Mexico are developed in a manner that is protective of both human health and the environment. The April 20, 2010, *Deepwater Horizon* incident raised serious questions about Interior's management of oil and gas activities in the Gulf of Mexico. Since the incident, Interior has fundamentally reorganized its oversight of offshore oil and gas activities through the creation of BSEE and BOEM. Interior has also enacted numerous policy changes intended to improve its oversight of offshore oil and gas activities. Moreover, Interior has taken and continues to take steps to reform its oversight. However, the ultimate effectiveness of Interior's reorganization and recent policy changes remains uncertain.

In particular, questions remain about one aspect of Interior's environmental NEPA analyses, which are required for exploration and development plans and play a critical role in assessing the potential effects of oil and gas development in the Gulf of Mexico. Interior completed a number of NEPA analyses without the most current, potentially relevant information—for example, in amendments to operator-submitted plans. Also, Interior technical staff reviewing the plans do not always coordinate with the agency's NEPA staff to ensure that any information included in subsequent amendments would not need to be considered as part of a NEPA analysis and do not always document such coordination. As a result, some of these NEPA analyses may have been based on incomplete or inaccurate information. Interior officials acknowledged that the controls in place are insufficient to prevent the approval of plans with NEPA analyses based on inaccurate or incomplete information. Without ensuring that NEPA analyses are conducted on complete and accurate information to analyze the potential effects of a proposed project as required by NEPA, Interior risks making an erroneous assessment of the environmental risks associated with such a project.

In addition, we are concerned with two limitations in Interior's exploration and development plan review process. First, because Interior's TIMS IT system does not include necessary data input controls, called edit checks, for preventing operators from submitting inaccurate and incomplete plans, Interior must devote resources to reviewing exploration and development plans for accuracy and completeness and asking operators to submit amendments to address inaccurate or incomplete plans. Interior attempted to develop an IT module called ePlans—which was to include edit checks—to help manage its review process for exploration and development plans; however, ePlans was never completed. Interior continues to evaluate ePlans and has worked on a requirements document for it. Second, because Interior's TIMS IT system does not have a field to collect information on (1) whether plan amendments were requested by Interior or initiated by the operator or (2) the reasons for the amendments, Interior management does not have the information it needs to conduct targeted outreach with operators on how to improve plan submissions, which could reduce the use of amendments as well as the burden on operators and Interior staff.

We are also concerned about the effectiveness of two aspects of Interior's inspection program. First, Interior has not assessed how new policy requirements, travel times to deepwater drilling rigs, and the current number of inspectors affect its ability to conduct drilling inspections; as a result, it cannot be certain that its informal monthly inspection goal is appropriate for overseeing drilling activities in the Gulf of Mexico. Furthermore, Interior's inspections routinely identify violations, but Interior's TIMS IT system is missing some data, such as the date that violations were found or corrected. As a result, Interior does not know on a real-time basis whether or when all violations were identified and corrected, potentially allowing unsafe conditions to continue for extended periods.

Additionally, Interior officials acknowledged challenges in maintaining timely regulations for drilling, especially as they relate to deepwater drilling. However, Interior has not systematically recorded operators' requests for departures from regulations in its TIMS IT system or whether the requests were approved or denied. Without data on departure requests, Interior is foregoing information that may help it to identify which regulations operators consistently request departures from and that it subsequently may use to identify when specific regulations should be considered for revision.

Furthermore, while Interior has taken steps to identify and evaluate drilling risks, its capacity to do so remains limited. Interior officials stated that they have the expertise to do so and acknowledged that such an effort could improve Interior's oversight of offshore oil and gas activities. Interior has taken some steps, for example, with its well containment screening tool, that can be used to evaluate overall well design based on risk. In this regard, even though operators are to report to Interior significant event data in weekly well activity reports once they begin drilling, Interior does not have clear definitions for some of these significant events, raising uncertainty as to whether Interior is systematically collecting and maintaining reliable data on risk factors associated with drilling operations. Moreover, some entities have expressed concern that Interior does not have a policy to categorize proposed drilling operations based on risk. For example, the report of the National Commission on the BP Deepwater Horizon Oil Spill and Offshore Drilling recommended that Interior should identify criteria and a methodology for assessing high-risk wells in collaboration with the U.S.

Geological Survey, the Department of Energy, NOAA, and academia and develop in-house competence to perform such sophisticated risk assessments. As the government faces significant financial constraints, without clear criteria and a methodology for assessing drilling operations according to risk, Interior may not adjust and evaluate its oversight—including inspections—in a cost-effective manner.

We and others have identified numerous opportunities for Interior to improve its oversight. Since the *Deepwater Horizon* incident, a number of government agencies, boards, and commissions have reported on the factors contributing to the incident and recommended areas for improvement. Interior has addressed and responded to the results of audits, as well as to many of the recommendations from these reports. However, Interior was unable to provide documentation that it was consistently tracking and responding to the results of external reviews—other than audits—to ensure that findings were promptly addressed and actions were taken to respond to recommendations until March 2012, when officials provided documentation that they had begun developing a database to track such recommendations. Without such tracking, it is uncertain whether Interior has fully considered and either concurred or disagreed with the findings of these reports and what, if any, steps it has taken to implement the recommendations it agrees with.

Questions also remain about Interior's efforts to complete long-term strategies for IT planning. Interior's IT systems are critical for managing its oil and gas oversight responsibilities. Recognizing this, Interior is taking steps to improve its implementation of IT projects and has identified IT system initiatives that could assist implementation of Interior's mission. However, it has not yet specified a time frame for when it would complete a comprehensive IT strategic plan, which should include results-oriented goals, strategies for achieving those goals, milestones, performance measures, and an analysis of interdependences among IT projects and activities, among other things. Without such a plan, BOEM and BSEE will have difficulty applying the lessons from prior failed improvement efforts and are at increased risk of falling short of meeting their system modernization goals.

In recent years, we have identified various challenges facing Interior in hiring, training, and retaining staff to oversee oil and gas activities. According to Interior officials, Interior historically did not provide standardized or rigorous training for its offshore inspection staff or engineers. Interior has taken steps to address the training gap by establishing a National Offshore Training and Learning Center, but

Interior officials stated that they are only at the initial phases of designing a curriculum. Additionally, Interior recently developed a succession plan for its regional offices, though Interior officials expressed concern that many critical positions are "one deep" and that, due to retirements, both BOEM and BSEE risk losing significant expertise and institutional knowledge. Finally, Interior continues to struggle to compete with industry in hiring qualified staff. Interior has taken steps to improve its human capital planning following *Deepwater Horizon,* but challenges remain. For example, Interior has not developed a comprehensive strategic workforce plan for both BOEM and BSEE that outlines specific strategies to address gaps in critical skills and competencies that need attention and processes to address human capital challenges, including determining the critical skills and competencies that will be needed to achieve current and future programmatic results. Since BOEM and BSEE started operations on October 1, 2011, neither has developed a strategic workforce plan, which could help guide each bureau's efforts to address human capital challenges and help guide future human capital management.

Finally, while Interior's implementing regulations for the OCS Lands Act require that the Secretary of the Interior provide for periodic consultation with stakeholders on a regional and national basis, Interior did not renew its OCS Policy Committee's charter for 2011. This long-standing advisory committee historically provided opportunities for stakeholders representing industry, conservation groups, and state and local governments to provide input to the Secretary on offshore leasing activities. Without this committee, or some equivalent alternative, opportunities for stakeholders to engage Interior on oil and gas leasing activities and other oil and gas related issues in the Gulf of Mexico have become more limited.

Recommendations for Executive Action

To improve Interior's oversight of offshore oil and gas activities in the Gulf of Mexico, we are making the following 11 recommendations to the Secretary of the Interior:

- Institute controls to help ensure that Interior's environmental NEPA analyses are based on the most current, relevant information, such as in amendments to operator-submitted exploration and development plans that would need to be considered as part of such an analysis.

- Continue to evaluate ePlans and develop edit checks to improve the accuracy and completeness of operators' exploration and development plan submissions.

- Track whether plan amendments were initiated at the request of Interior or the operator and, for amendments initiated at the request of Interior, the reasons for the amendments to provide Interior's managers with information needed to conduct targeted outreach with operators on how to improve plan submissions and reduce the use of amendments.

- Enhance the effectiveness of Interior's inspection program by

  - assessing how new inspection policy requirements, travel times to drilling rigs, and numbers of inspectors affect Interior's ability to conduct monthly drilling inspections and whether its monthly inspection goal is appropriate; and

  - ensuring that both violations and correction dates are recorded in Interior's TIMS IT system in a timely manner.

- Ensure that operators' requests, approvals, and disapprovals for departure from regulations are recorded to provide Interior with information that would better allow it to identify when specific regulations should be considered for revision.

- Enhance Interior's capacity for identifying and evaluating offshore oil and gas drilling operations according to risk, thereby allowing it to adjust and evaluate its oversight accordingly by (1) identifying and systematically collecting and maintaining reliable data on risk factors associated with drilling operations, (2) providing operators with clear definitions for significant events in the weekly well activity reports and developing a way to characterize and record these events systematically and reliably, and (3) using the risk factors and significant events data to develop a risk-based approach with clear criteria to prospectively evaluate and categorize drilling operations according to risk and retrospectively to evaluate the performance of oversight and risk mitigation activities in avoiding significant events.

- Complete and maintain its database for tracking recommendations, so that Interior consistently tracks and responds to the results of all audits and other external reviews to ensure that findings are promptly addressed and appropriate actions are taken to respond to recommendations and improve oversight.

- Direct BOEM and BSEE to set milestones and a completion date for developing a comprehensive IT strategic plan, including results-oriented goals, strategies, milestones, performance measures, and an

GAO-12-423 Oil and Gas Management

analysis of interdependencies among projects and activities, and use this plan to guide and coordinate their modernization goals.

- Direct BOEM and BSEE to develop a strategic workforce plan that, among other actions, determines the critical skills and competencies that will be needed to achieve current and future programmatic results and develop strategies to address gaps and human capital conditions in critical skills and competencies that need attention.

- Consider reinstating the OCS Policy Committee, on a regional and national basis, or adopt an equivalent alternative to allow increased opportunities for stakeholders to provide input as it relates to offshore oil and gas leasing activities to ensure Interior fulfills its obligations under the implementing regulations of the OCS Lands Act.

Agency Comments and Our Evaluation

We provided a draft of this report to Interior for review and comment. Interior generally agreed with our findings and recommendations.

Interior also provided its own analysis of exploration and development plan and drilling permit review times which differed from our analysis in two ways. First, our analysis included plans and permits submitted and approved within each separate time frame, while Interior's analysis required only that the plan was submitted and approved, regardless of the time frame. Second, our analysis of review times included data through September 30, 2011, while Interior's analysis included data through May 31, 2012, allowing time for Interior staff and operators to become more familiar with the increased environmental and safety requirements and new review process.

While we believe our analysis provides a more conservative and accurate view of review times, Interior's analysis is not incorrect for examining trends in review times for plans and permits. Further, Interior's analysis provides a more current assessment of review times in the post *Deepwater Horizon* incident period. Overall, Interior's analyses found that review times for plans and permits has decreased since the *Deepwater Horizon* incident, which is consistent with the results of our work.

Interior and the Department of Commerce (NOAA) also provided technical comments which we incorporated as appropriate. Appendix IV contains Interior's comment letter and enclosure containing its analysis of plan and permit review times.

As agreed with your offices, unless you publicly announce the contents of this report earlier, we plan no further distribution until 30 days from the report date. At that time, we will send copies to the Secretary of the Interior, the Secretary of Commerce, the appropriate congressional committees, and other interested parties. In addition, the report will be available at no charge on the GAO website at http://www.gao.gov.

If you or your staff members have any questions about this report, please contact me at (202) 512-3841 or ruscof@gao.gov. Contact points for our Offices of Congressional Relations and Public Affairs may be found on the last page of this report. GAO staff who made key contributions to this report are listed in appendix V.

Frank Rusco
Director, Natural Resources
    and Environment

Appendix I: Scope and Methodology

This report examines (1) Interior's reorganization of its oversight of offshore oil and gas activities in the Gulf of Mexico since the *Deepwater Horizon* incident; (2) how key policy changes Interior has implemented since this incident have affected Interior's National Environmental Policy Act (NEPA) analyses, plans reviews, and drilling permit reviews; (3) the extent to which Interior's inspections of Gulf of Mexico drilling rigs and production platforms identified violations or resulted in civil penalty assessments, and how key policy changes since this incident have affected Interior's inspection and civil penalties program; (4) when stakeholders have provided input to Interior about proposed offshore oil and gas activities, and the extent to which stakeholders believe Interior considered such input from approximately 2002 through January 2012; and (5) key challenges, if any, affecting Interior's oversight of offshore oil and gas activities in the Gulf of Mexico following its reorganization.

To identify the actions Interior has taken as part of its reorganization of Interior's Minerals Management Service (MMS), we reviewed relevant regulations, Interior's secretarial orders as well as applicable federal rules associated with the reorganization. We also interviewed knowledgeable officials at Interior's headquarters office in Washington, D.C., and its Gulf of Mexico regional office in New Orleans, including staff overseeing the reorganization. We reviewed previous and current budget documentation detailing changes to the MMS; the Bureau of Ocean Energy Management, Regulation, and Enforcement (BOEMRE); the Bureau of Ocean Energy Management; and the Bureau of Safety and Environmental Enforcement. We also reviewed documentation and guidance developed by both Interior and an outside consultant hired by Interior to guide the reorganization, such as by establishing time frames and other milestones. We also reviewed documentation including memoranda of understanding, memoranda of agreements, and standard operating procedures used to define working relationships following the reorganization's completion, as well as supporting documentation used to develop these documents. Additionally, we met with Interior officials at their headquarters' offices in Herndon, Virginia, and Washington, D.C., and at the Gulf of Mexico regional office in New Orleans, to discuss these documents. Due to the short amount of time that elapsed since the reorganization, we did not evaluate the effect of the reorganization on Interior's ability to conduct oversight of oil and gas activities in the Gulf of Mexico.

To examine key policy changes Interior has implemented since the *Deepwater Horizon* incident related to overseeing oil and gas development in the Gulf of Mexico, and how these changes have affected

Interior's operations, we reviewed agency documents relevant to Interior's work with NEPA exploration and development plans, and drilling permits. We also interviewed officials from Interior's Gulf of Mexico regional office and New Orleans and Lafayette district offices. We analyzed Interior data from its Technical Information Management (TIMS) information technology (IT) system on NEPA reviews and exploration and development plan approvals from January 1, 2000, through September 30, 2011. We analyzed Interior data from its TIMS IT system on drilling permit approvals from January 1, 2005, through September 30, 2011. Our review of drilling permits was limited to data beginning in 2005 due to concerns about the reliability of data recorded prior to 2005. We assessed the reliability of these data by (1) reviewing documentation about the data and the system that produced them; (2) interviewing agency officials knowledgeable about the data; and (3) verifying our results with agency officials. Based on this assessment, we found these data sufficiently reliable for our purposes. Because many policy changes are still under way and have not been in place long enough to evaluate, our report does not evaluate the effectiveness of the policy changes to reduce the risk associated with offshore oil and gas activities.

To determine the extent to which Interior's inspections resulted in violations and penalties and how key policy changes since the *Deepwater Horizon* incident have affected Interior's inspection and civil penalties program, we analyzed Interior's inspection and civil penalty data from its TIMS IT system from January 1, 2000, through September 30, 2011. We assessed the reliability of these data by (1) reviewing documentation about the data and the system that produced them; (2) interviewing agency officials knowledgeable about the data; and (3) verifying our results with agency officials. Based on this assessment, we found these data sufficiently reliable for our purposes. We also reviewed agency documents relevant to Interior's inspection and civil penalty program and interviewed officials from Interior's headquarters office in Herndon, VA, the Gulf of Mexico regional office, and the Houma district office. Because many of these policy changes are still under way and have not been in place long enough to evaluate, we did not evaluate the effectiveness of the policy changes to reduce the risk associated with offshore oil and gas activities in this report.

To determine when stakeholders provided input to Interior about proposed offshore oil and gas activities and the extent to which they believe Interior considered and addressed their input (the Fish and Wildlife Service, the National Oceanic and Atmospheric Administration, coastal states, industry and conservation groups) on oil and gas development in the Gulf of Mexico from 2002 through January 2012, we reviewed relevant federal statutes on Interior's process for offshore oil and gas development. Key statutes included the Outer Continental Shelf Lands Act, National Environmental Policy Act, the Endangered Species Act, the Marine Mammal Protection Act, the Magnuson-Stevens Fishery Conservation and Management Act, and the Coastal Zone Management Act. We identified key lease sale documents for the Gulf of Mexico from 2000 through January 2012, and limited our review to the 5-year Gulf of Mexico Outer Continental Shelf (OCS) multilease sale environmental impact statements (EIS) documents and individual lease sale EIS documents that were not included within Interior's 5-year plan. We identified and interviewed both government and nongovernment stakeholders that collaborated or submitted input to Interior concerning offshore oil and gas activities during the period of our review. Government stakeholders included officials from the Department of Commerce's National Oceanic and Atmospheric Administration (NOAA) and Interior's Fish and Wildlife Service (FWS) and state environmental agencies responsible for conducting consistency reviews under the Coastal Zone Management Act (CZMA) in Alabama, Florida, Louisiana, Mississippi, and Texas. We collected correspondence documentation between stakeholders and Interior and interviewed officials from NOAA and FWS to determine whether and when they submitted input on oil and gas NEPA documents. We also interviewed officials from the five Gulf of Mexico coastal states (Alabama, Florida, Louisiana, Mississippi, and Texas) to determine when and how they provided input to interior on proposed offshore oil and gas activities. Nongovernment stakeholders included representatives from conservation organizations and the associations representing the offshore oil and gas industry. Conservation organizations were selected based on the following criteria: (1) they were involved in environmental issues specific to the Gulf of Mexico, (2) they were referred to us by a representative from a conservation group that we initially interviewed, and (3) time and resource constraints. We selected three oil and gas industry trade groups based on their announcement to form oil spill task forces and because each represents a minimum of 250 companies in the oil and gas industry. GAO spoke to representatives of two of the three trade groups. Despite several attempts to speak to the third, our correspondence was not returned. The findings from our interviews cannot be generalized to groups we did not speak with.

To determine what challenges, if any, Interior faces in providing oversight of offshore oil and gas activities in the Gulf of Mexico, we reviewed relevant laws, regulations, and Interior guidance and documentation, and interviewed knowledgeable officials in Interior's headquarters and Gulf of

Mexico regional offices. We also reviewed our previous work on Interior as well as federal external reviews that reported on factors contributing to the *Deepwater Horizon* incident. To report on Interior's ability to identify and evaluate drilling risk, we obtained Interior data from its TIMS IT system on significant events from January 1, 2004, through May 14, 2011, but determined that the data was not sufficiently reliable for our purposes. We also reviewed documentation and interviewed Interior officials responsible for overseeing drilling permit reviews and drilling rig inspections. To further our understanding of IT challenges, we reviewed Interior's IT strategic plans, as well as budget and other documentation describing Interior's implementation of IT systems. We also spoke with knowledgeable Interior officials responsible for overseeing IT systems as well as officials with direct experience working with these systems. To enhance our understanding of human capital issues, we reviewed Interior's human capital strategic plans developed for MMS, as well as other human capital documentation and reviewed data provided to us by Interior, and verified the reliability of the data for our purposes by reviewing documentation and gathering information from people knowledgeable of the system. We also met with Interior officials responsible for overseeing human capital planning in the Gulf of Mexico regional office. To report on Interior's responses to federal government stakeholders, we reviewed federal government stakeholder studies and Interior's responses and discussed this documentation with the responsible interior official. To further our review of the development of federal regulations, we reviewed Interior documentation on regulations and met with knowledgeable Interior officials and representatives from the American Petroleum Institute to obtain their views. To enhance our understanding of the effect, if any, of resource constraints on Interior's oversight, we reviewed relevant budgetary documentation from Interior and met with Interior officials in headquarters and the Gulf of Mexico to discuss these issues.

We conducted this performance audit from September 2010 to July 2012 in accordance with generally accepted government auditing standards. Those standards require that we plan and perform the audit to obtain sufficient, appropriate evidence to provide a reasonable basis for our findings and conclusions based on our audit objectives. We believe that the evidence obtained provides a reasonable basis for our findings and conclusions based on our audit.

Appendix II: Interior's Organizational Structures for the Bureau of Ocean Energy Management and the Bureau of Safety and Environmental Enforcement

The Bureau of Ocean Energy Management's and the Bureau of Safety and Environmental Enforcement's detailed organizational structures are provided in figures 17 and 18.

Figure 17: Bureau of Ocean Energy Management Organizational Structure

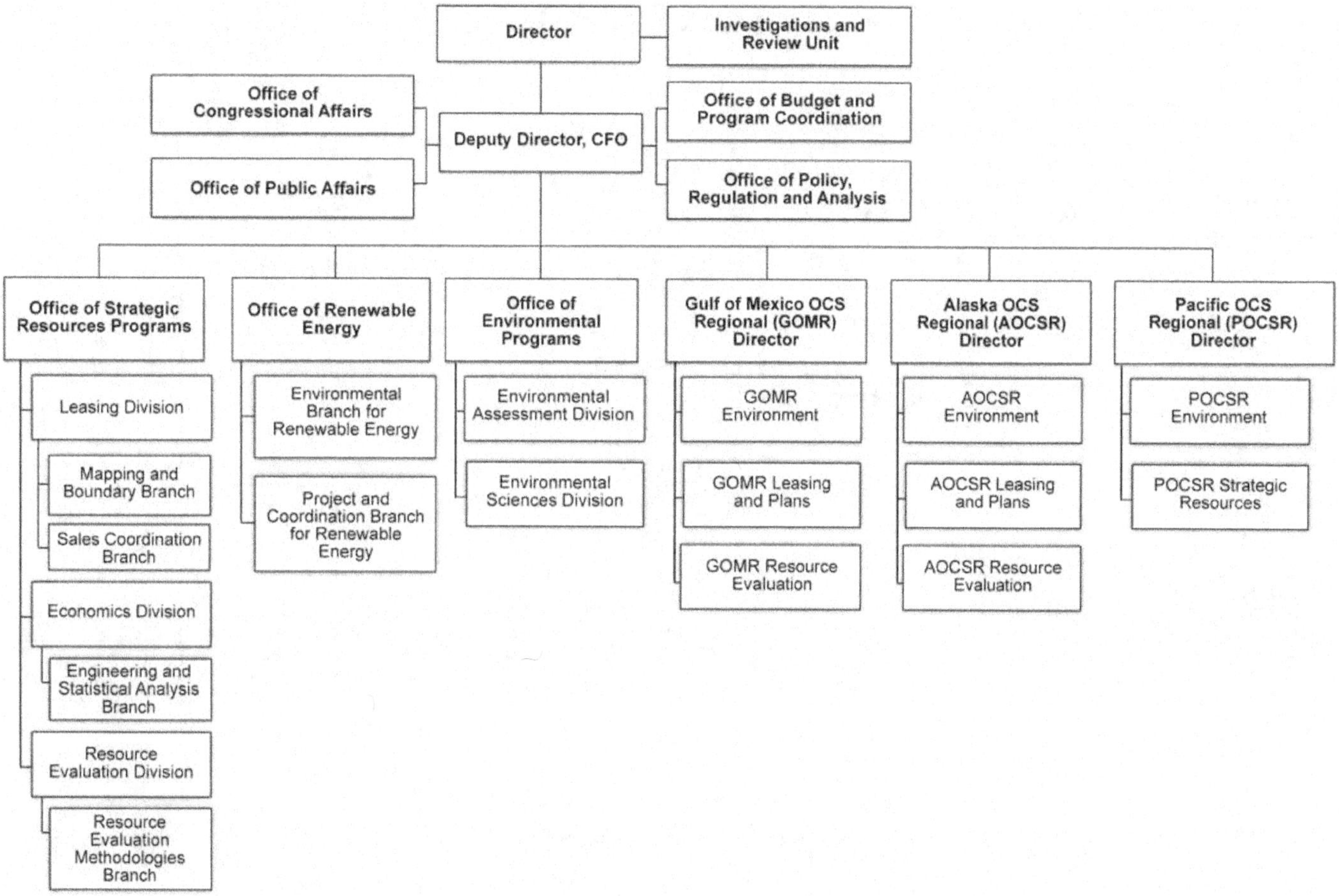

Source: Bureau of Ocean Energy Management (BOEM).

Appendix II: Interior's Organizational
Structures for the Bureau of Ocean Energy
Management and the Bureau of Safety and
Environmental Enforcement

Figure 18: Bureau of Safety and Environmental Enforcement Organizational Structure

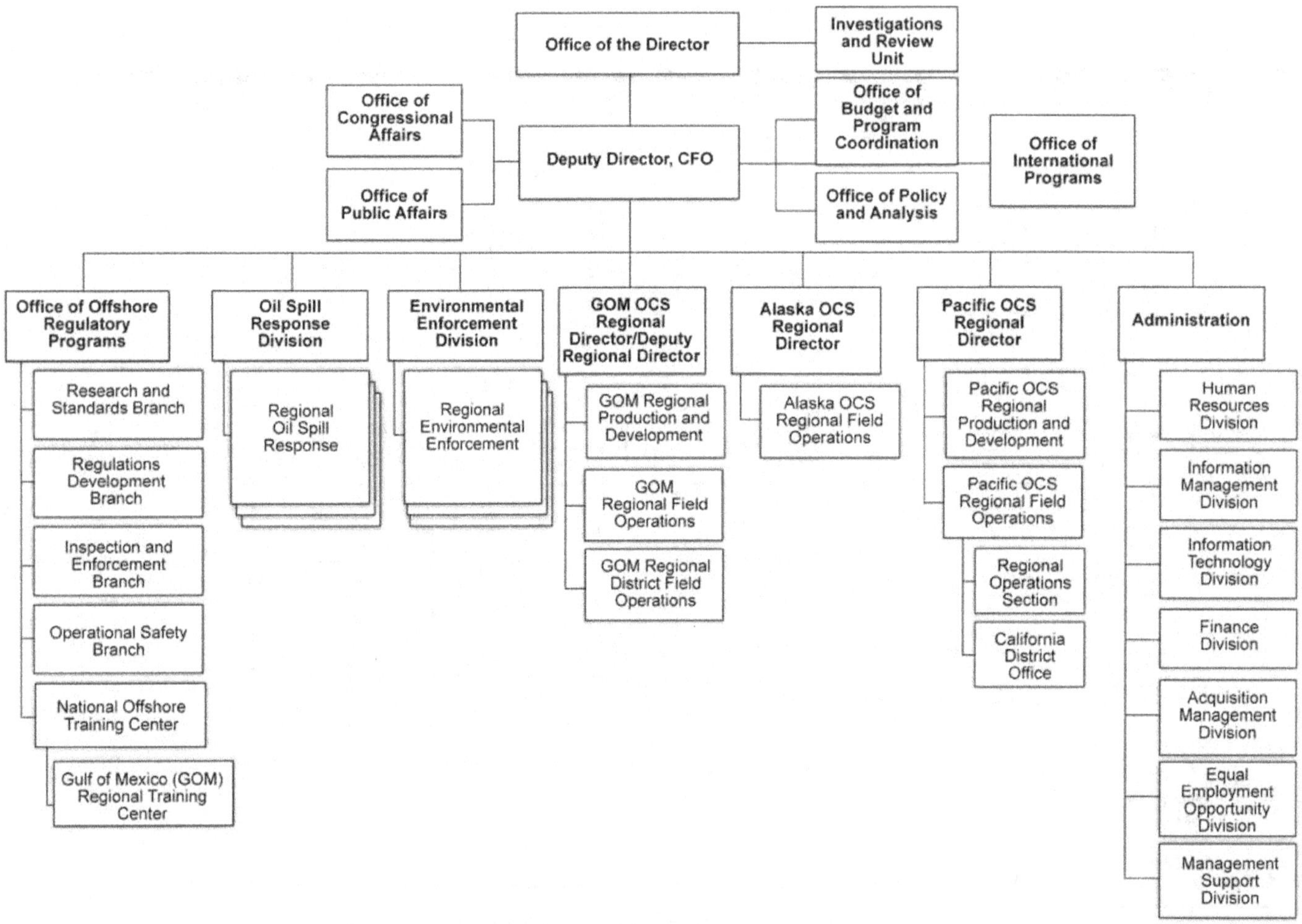

Source: Bureau of Safety and Environmental Enforcement (BSEE).

Appendix III: Federal and State Stakeholder Input to Interior's Proposed Gulf of Mexico Oil and Gas Activities for 2002 through 2012

Federal stakeholders—the National Oceanic and Atmospheric Administration (NOAA) and Fish and Wildlife Service (FWS)—and state government stakeholders provide input to Interior through a variety of legal authorities.

NOAA

According to NOAA officials, NOAA generally provided its most substantive input to Interior while Interior was developing its Gulf of Mexico multilease sale environmental impact statement (EIS). Table 7 outlines NOAA's input to Interior.

Table 7: NOAA's Input to Interior's Gulf of Mexico Outer Continental Shelf (OCS) Lease Sale Environmental Impact Statement (EIS) National Environmental Policy Act (NEPA) documents, 2002—2012

	National Environmental Policy Act	Endangered Species Act	Magnuson-Stevens Fishery Conservation and Management Act	Marine Mammal Protection Act
Gulf of Mexico Lease Sale EIS Documents Prior to the *Deepwater Horizon* Incident				
Final Gulf of Mexico OCS 2003-2007 Multilease Sale EIS (November 2002)	Yes – informal	Yes – biological opinion, November 29, 2002	Yes – Letter documenting consultation April 29, 2002	No
Final Gulf of Mexico OCS Lease Sales 189 and 197 Eastern Planning Area EIS (May 2003)[a]	Yes – informal	Yes – biological opinion, August 30, 2003	Yes – Letter documenting consultation November 19, 2002	No
Final Gulf of Mexico OCS 2007 – 2012 Multilease Sale EIS (April 2007)	Yes – informal	Yes – biological opinion, June 29, 2007	Yes – Letter documenting consultation December 21, 2006	No
Final Gulf of Mexico OCS Lease Sale 224 Eastern Planning Area Supplemental EIS (October 2007)[a]	Yes – informal	Yes – biological opinion, June 15, 2001. Still in effect. Interior expanded lease area 181 after the biological opinion was completed. Interior requested NOAA review of the amended action. On October 9, 2007, NOAA determined that the expanded area would not change the effects to listed species already considered, and would be covered under the existing biological opinion.	Yes - Letter Documenting Consultation July 19, 2007	No
Final Gulf of Mexico OCS Supplemental 2009 – 2012 Supplemental EIS (September 2008)[b]	No	Yes – biological opinion, June 29, 2007. Still in effect.	Yes – Letter documenting consultation December 13, 2006.	No

Appendix III: Federal and State Stakeholder
Input to Interior's Proposed Gulf of Mexico Oil
and Gas Activities for 2002 through 2012

	National Environmental Policy Act	Endangered Species Act	Magnuson-Stevens Fishery Conservation and Management Act	Marine Mammal Protection Act
Gulf of Mexico Lease Sale EIS Documents After the *Deepwater Horizon* Incident				
Final Gulf of Mexico OCS Lease Sale 218 Western Planning Area Supplemental EIS (August 2011)[c]	Yes – formal, June 6, 2011	Yes – Interior requested reinitiation of the Endangered Species Act Consultation on July 30, 2010, and NOAA responded on September 24, 2010. Reinitiations are not complete. The June 29, 2007, biological opinion remains in effect until the reinitiated consultations are complete.	Yes – Letter Documenting Consultation June 6, 2011. Post-*Deepwater Horizon* incident, NOAA requested a comprehensive review of existing EFH consultations on September 24, 2010. NOAA and Interior are working on a new consultation document for the 2012-2017 multisale EIS.	No
Final Gulf of Mexico OCS Lease Sale 216 and 222 Central Planning Area Supplemental EIS (January 2012)[c]	Yes – formal, August 15, 2011	Yes – Interior requested reinitiation of Endangered Species Act Consultation on July 30, 2010, and NOAA responded on September 24, 2010. Reinitiations are not complete. The June 29, 2007 biological opinion remains in effect until the reinitiated consultations are complete.	Yes – Letter Documenting Consultation August 15, 2011. Post-*Deepwater Horizon* incident, NOAA requested a comprehensive review of existing essential fish habitat consultations on September 24, 2010. NOAA and Interior are working on a new consultation document for the 2012-2017 multisale EIS	No

Source: GAO's analysis of Interior and NOAA documents and input from NOAA officials.

[a]Interior does not include lease sales that could affect the eastern planning area in its programmatic Gulf of Mexico multilease sale EIS documents; rather, it prepares a separate lease sale EIS.

[b]Interior had to supplement its programmatic Gulf of Mexico 2007-2012 multilease sale EIS because of the Gulf of Mexico Energy Security Act of 2006.

[c]Interior created a separate lease sale EIS due to potential changes in the baseline conditions that may have occurred since the *Deepwater Horizon* incident.

National Environmental Policy Act. NOAA officials stated that they do not always submit formal comments under NEPA on Interior's Gulf of Mexico multilease sale EIS or individual lease sale EIS documents, but generally provide comments informally under other legal authorities, such as the ESA. Our analysis of Interior's Gulf of Mexico lease sale environmental impact statement (EIS) documents from 2002 through January 2012 found that NOAA did not formally comment on the five draft lease sale EIS documents completed prior to the *Deepwater Horizon* incident. NOAA officials explained that, in the past, they generally consulted informally with Interior as it developed its Gulf of Mexico multilease sale EIS documents and individual lease sale EIS documents so that NOAA could ensure that the information necessary to complete its consultations were

Appendix III: Federal and State Stakeholder
Input to Interior's Proposed Gulf of Mexico Oil
and Gas Activities for 2002 through 2012

included in Interior's National Environmental Policy Act (NEPA) documents. However, NOAA provided comments on the supplemental EIS documents for both the Western and Central Planning areas—the first lease sale NEPA documents completed since the *Deepwater Horizon* incident—indicating a shift in its practice.[1]

NOAA officials also explained that, with regard to other Interior NEPA documents, such as individual lease sale environmental assessments (EA) or NEPA analyses associated with exploration and development plans and drilling permits, as long as the environmental conditions had not changed since the completion of the Gulf of Mexico multilease sale EIS or individual lease sale EIS, and the exploration and development plans or drilling permits were approved with the stated mitigation requirements, NOAA typically has not requested or received these documents and therefore generally has not commented on them.

Endangered Species Act. NOAA officials told us that they generally rely on information included in Interior's draft Gulf of Mexico multilease sale EIS documents to prepare biological opinions required under Section 7 of the Endangered Species Act (ESA).[2] NOAA officials further explained that the time frames covered by the biological opinions generally coincide with time frames analyzed in the Gulf of Mexico multilease sale EIS documents. For example, NOAA's biological opinion dated November 29, 2002, covers all proposed activities analyzed in Interior's draft Gulf of Mexico OCS 2003-2007 multilease sale EIS, which was finalized in November 2002. NOAA officials told us that by providing input informally through the NEPA process and formally through ESA Section 7 consultations, they have ensured that Interior's final Gulf of Mexico multilease sale EIS and other NEPA documents included any necessary mitigation measures—such as Notices to Lessees and Operators or lease stipulations—to protect threatened or engendered species. Accordingly, all subsequent approvals of oil and gas activities, including exploration and development plans and drilling permits, would be tiered back to the final Gulf of Mexico multilease sale EIS. Although NOAA officials told us they typically do not request or receive

---

[1]While the leases included in this lease sale were previously analyzed in the Final Programmatic Gulf of Mexico OCS Supplemental EIS 2009-2012 Multilease Sale (September 2008), the potential effects of the *Deepwater Horizon* incident caused Interior to prepare an EIS, taking into consideration new information.

[2]Interior officials stated that they also provided Biological Assessments in addition to the EIS for consideration in the Section 7 analysis.

Appendix III: Federal and State Stakeholder
Input to Interior's Proposed Gulf of Mexico Oil
and Gas Activities for 2002 through 2012

these documents from Interior and, therefore, do not typically comment on them as it relates to their authority under the ESA, recent coordination between NOAA and Interior has resulted in interim ESA consultation procedures. According to NOAA officials, these procedures, finalized on February 8, 2012, ensure that the existing mitigation measures in the biological opinion are sufficient. As a result, NOAA officials told us that Interior is now consulting with them on both exploration and development plans, among other items. These interim procedures will remain in place until they are replaced with new mitigation measures and procedures in a new biological opinion under the ESA.

Our analysis of NOAA's biological opinions for the lease sales we reviewed found that, prior to the *Deepwater Horizon* incident, NOAA completed four biological opinions, all of which found that the proposed lease sales and their associated actions were not likely to jeopardize the continued existence of any endangered or threatened species under NOAA's jurisdiction. These biological opinions included both mandatory terms and conditions for Interior, in addition to discretionary recommendations intended to minimize or avoid adverse effects of proposed actions on listed species and critical habitat. Exceptions to this process exist, for example, if certain new information becomes available during the time period for which the biological opinion is in effect, such as with the *Deepwater Horizon* incident, Interior is required to reinitiate ESA Section 7 consultations. On July 30, 2010, Interior requested reinitiation of Section 7 ESA consultation with NOAA as it prepared supplemental NEPA documents for the remaining lease sales initially included in the final programmatic Gulf of Mexico OCS 2007-2012 multilease sale EIS (April 2007). In the interim, the existing July 29, 2007, biological opinion will remain in effect.

Magnuson-Stevens Fishery Conservation and Management Act. NOAA generally uses information included in Interior's draft Gulf of Mexico multilease sale EIS to facilitate its consultation requirements under the Magnuson-Stevens Fishery Conservation and Management Act. Specifically, NOAA works with Interior to ensure that the elements of Essential Fish Habitat assessments required by regulation are included in Interior's Gulf of Mexico multilease sale EIS. Then, similar to NOAA's biological opinions, NOAA's Essential Fish Habitat programmatic consultations remain in effect for the time period of the Interior lease program being analyzed in the final Gulf of Mexico multilease sale EIS. For example, NOAA's Essential Fish Habitat programmatic consultation letter dated April 26, 2002, covers activities associated with Interior's final Gulf of Mexico OCS 2003-2007 multilease sale EIS, dated November

Appendix III: Federal and State Stakeholder
Input to Interior's Proposed Gulf of Mexico Oil
and Gas Activities for 2002 through 2012

Chronology of NOAA's and Interior's Effort to Examine Effects of Oil and Gas Seismic Activities on Marine Mammals

Since 2002, NOAA has been working with Interior on whether and how to issue take authorizations for marine mammals resulting from seismic activities, but the issue remains unresolved. In 2002, Interior requested, pursuant to the MMPA, that NOAA authorize the take of sperm whales incidental to seismic surveys during oil and gas exploration activities in the Gulf of Mexico. On July 30, 2004, to support its application, Interior completed its final programmatic EA and released the document for public comment. However, on September 29, 2004, Interior revised its initial request to include dolphins, beaked whales, and Bryde's whales. NOAA determined that Interior's EA was insufficient for assessing the potential effects of seismic activities on the marine mammals included in Interior's revised application and concluded that an EIS was necessary to identify the potential effects of seismic technologies on marine mammals.

NOAA elected to serve as the lead agency for preparing the EIS, with assistance from Interior, but did not begin working on the analysis until 2006. NOAA officials said that significant delays occurred because (1) Interior was also preparing a draft EIS examining seismic effects in the Arctic, which was a higher priority; (2) NOAA had difficulty obtaining the seismic data from industry necessary for its analysis; and (3) NOAA had very limited staff available to work on the analysis. Since 2002, Interior has worked with NOAA to develop interim mitigation measures designed to protect marine mammals, such as issuing a Notice to Lessees and Operators requiring them to have visual observers present to watch for marine mammals when conducting seismic activities.

2002. Also, similar to NOAA's biological opinions, the consultation letter may include recommendations to minimize and avoid the effects of oil and gas development on Essential Fish Habitats. For example, NOAA and Interior cooperatively developed a mitigation measure for the protection of certain organisms that inhabit the seafloor of the Gulf of Mexico.

Our analysis of NOAA's Essential Fish Habitat consultations from approximately 2002 through January 2012 found that, prior to the *Deepwater Horizon* incident, NOAA completed five consultations, all of which, according to NOAA officials, found that if the proposed Interior mitigations, conservation recommendations, and standard lease stipulations and regulations are followed, the effects on Essential Fish Habitats resulting from activities proposed in the lease sale EIS documents would be minimal. However, after the *Deepwater Horizon* incident, NOAA requested a comprehensive review of existing essential fish habitat consultations on September 24, 2010.[3] NOAA and Interior are working on a new consultation document for Interior's next Gulf of Mexico multilease sale EIS.

Marine Mammal Protection Act. Under the Marine Mammal Protection Act (MMPA), Interior coordinates with NOAA to mitigate potentially negative effects on marine mammals and obtain authorizations if mammals are likely to be taken. NOAA officials stated that NOAA worked with Interior through the ESA and NEPA processes to institute lease stipulations and Notices to Lessees and Operators that provide protection for threatened or endangered marine mammals. However, both NOAA and Interior officials acknowledged that adverse effects to marine mammals (both ESA-listed and nonlisted) from seismic surveys in the Gulf of Mexico could occur and that an MMPA authorization would be appropriate and, as a result, Interior first applied for an MMPA authorization in 2002. NOAA and Interior have been working toward the issuance of MMPA incidental take regulations to cover seismic surveys in the Gulf of Mexico. Since 2002, however, changes in the anticipated activities, the need for

---

[3]NOAA officials stated that to the extent that Interior can examine the effects to essential fish habitat and related critical habitat for ESA-listed species together (or at least keep the potential effects in mind as they complete their NEPA documentation and related ESA documentation), it will aid their overall analysis from the standpoint of ecosystem effects and, potentially, regulatory compliance under the ESA and Magnusson-Stevens Fishery Conservation and Management Act.

Appendix III: Federal and State Stakeholder
Input to Interior's Proposed Gulf of Mexico Oil
and Gas Activities for 2002 through 2012

NEPA analyses, and resource limitations have slowed down the process and regulations have not yet been issued.

In April 2011, Interior again revised its application for take authorizations based on industries' updated seismic effort projections, which NOAA later published for comment. However, the EIS is not still complete, and NOAA has issued no take authorizations for marine mammals for seismic activities. In addition, a group of conservation organizations filed a number of formal notices of intent to sue the Secretary of the Interior and, in one case, the Secretary of Commerce, for failure to comply with MMPA and ESA when approving offshore oil and gas activities in the Gulf of Mexico. For example, in its February 9, 2011, notice, the group informed Interior and NOAA that it intended to challenge the 10 projects approved since October 15, 2010, for, among other things, failing to obtain take permits under the MMPA and ESA that are designed to protect endangered species and marine mammals, such as whales, from harmful offshore oil activities.

FWS

According to FWS officials, FWS also generally provided its most substantive input while Interior was developing its Gulf of Mexico multilease sale EIS documents. Table 8 outlines FWS's input to Interior.

Table 8: FWS's Input to Interior's Gulf of Mexico OCS Lease Sale EIS NEPA documents, 2002-2012

	National Environmental Policy Act	Endangered Species Act
Gulf of Mexico Lease Sale EIS Documents Prior to the _Deepwater Horizon_ Incident		
Final Gulf of Mexico OCS 2003-2007 Multilease Sale EIS (November 2002)	Yes – informal	Yes – biological opinion, January 13, 2003
Final Gulf of Mexico OCS Lease Sales 189 and 197 Eastern Planning Area EIS (May 2003)[a]	Yes – formal, January 27, 2003	Yes – biological opinion, August, 2003
Final Gulf of Mexico OCS 2007 – 2012 Multilease Sale EIS (April 2007)	Yes – formal, January 5, 2007	Yes – concurrence to Interior's biological assessment September 14, 2007
Final Gulf of Mexico OCS Lease Lease Sale 224 Eastern Planning Area Supplemental EIS (October 2007)[a]	Yes – Informal	Yes – biological opinion, June 8, 2001
Final Gulf of Mexico OCS Supplemental 2009 – 2012 Supplemental EIS (September 2008)[b]	Yes – formal, June 6, 2008	Yes – concurrence to Interior's original biological assessment September 14, 2007. Concur to draft Supplemental EIS (addition of Lease Sale 181 and updates) via e-mail dated July 30, 2008.

Appendix III: Federal and State Stakeholder
Input to Interior's Proposed Gulf of Mexico Oil
and Gas Activities for 2002 through 2012

	National Environmental Policy Act	Endangered Species Act
Gulf of Mexico Multilease Sale EIS Documents After the *Deepwater Horizon* Incident		
Final Gulf of Mexico OCS Lease Sale 218 Western Planning Area Supplemental EIS (August 2011)[c]	Yes – formal, June 6, 2011	Yes – Interior requested reinitiation of ESA consultations on July 30, 2010, and FWS responded on September 27, 2010. Reinitiations are not complete. The September 14, 2007 and July 30, 2008 concurrence to Interior's biological assessments remain in effect until the reinitiated consultations are complete
Final Gulf of Mexico OCS Lease Sale 216 and 222 Central Planning Area Supplemental EIS (January 2012)[c]	Yes – formal, August 10, 2011	Yes – Interior requested reinitiation of ESA consultations on July 30, 2010, and FWS responded on September 27, 2010. Reinitiations are not complete. The September 14, 2007 and July 30, 2008 concurrence to Interior's biological assessments remain in effect until the reinitiated consultations are complete

Source: GAO analysis of Interior and FWS documents and input from FWS officials.

[a]Due to the drilling moratorium in the eastern planning area of the Gulf of Mexico, Interior does not include lease sales that could affect the eastern planning area in its programmatic Gulf of Mexico multilease sale EIS documents; rather, it prepares a separate lease sale EIS.

[b]Interior had to supplement its programmatic Gulf of Mexico 2007-2012 multilease sale EIS because of the Gulf of Mexico Security Act of 2006.

[c]Interior created a separate lease sale EIS due to potential changes in the baseline conditions that may have occurred since the *Deepwater Horizon* incident.

National Environmental Policy Act. FWS officials told us that they are generally involved with Interior as it develops its Gulf of Mexico multilease sale EIS. Similar to NOAA, FWS officials told us they coordinate with Interior early in the process and are able to provide information on endangered species necessary to ensure that Interior meets its ESA requirements.

Our analysis of Interior's Gulf of Mexico lease sale EIS documents from 2002 through January 2012 indicated that FWS provided formal comments to Interior on three of the five draft lease sale EIS documents prior to the *Deepwater Horizon* incident and on both draft lease EIS documents since the incident. FWS officials also explained that, again, like NOAA, because they provide their most substantive input during the lease sale planning process as Interior develops a Gulf of Mexico multilease sale EIS, they do not typically formally comment on postlease

Appendix III: Federal and State Stakeholder
Input to Interior's Proposed Gulf of Mexico Oil
and Gas Activities for 2002 through 2012

activities, including lease sale EA documents,[4] exploration and development plans, or individual drilling permits.

Endangered Species Act. FWS officials told us that, until 2007, FWS typically relied on information included in the draft Gulf of Mexico multilease sale EIS to complete the required ESA Section 7 consultations.[5] Similar to NOAA, FWS officials explained that the time frames covered by these consultations—which resulted in biological opinions drafted by FWS—generally coincided with time frames analyzed in Interior's final Gulf of Mexico multilease sale EIS. For example, FWS's biological opinion dated January 13, 2003, covers the proposed activities analyzed in Interior's draft Gulf of Mexico OCS 2003-2007 multilease sale EIS, which was finalized in November 2002. Our analysis of FWS's ESA consultations from 2002 through 2012 found that, prior to the *Deepwater Horizon* incident; FWS completed three ESA Section 7 consultations, all of which found that the proposed lease sales and their associated actions were not likely to adversely affect any threatened or endangered species. FWS prepared a biological opinion at the request of Interior that found that the proposed lease sales were not likely to jeopardize the continued existence of any endangered or threatened species.

Beginning in 2007, instead of formally consulting with Interior and preparing a biological opinion for the final Gulf of Mexico OCS 2007-2012 multilease sale EIS (April 2007), FWS requested that it informally consult with Interior and that Interior prepare a biological assessment.[6] FWS officials explained that formal consultations resulting in biological opinions were resource intensive but generally necessary to determine if the authorized incidental take would jeopardize a threatened or endangered species. However, in 2007, based on the outcomes of the previously completed biological opinions which all concluded that Interior's proposed actions were not likely

---

[4]FWS officials told us that they sometimes informally consult with Interior on individual lease sales.

[5]Interior officials stated that they also provided Biological Assessments in addition to the EIS for consideration in the Section 7 analysis.

[6]Under Section 7, federal agencies must consult with FWS when any action the agency carries out, funds, or authorizes—such as through a permit—may affect a listed endangered or threatened species or critical habitat. This process usually begins as informal consultation. When a federal agency determines that, through a biological assessment or other review, its action is likely to adversely affect a listed species, the agency submits a request to FWS for a formal consultation.

Appendix III: Federal and State Stakeholder
Input to Interior's Proposed Gulf of Mexico Oil
and Gas Activities for 2002 through 2012

to adversely affect listed species, FWS requested that Interior consider completing the consultation informally, rather than formally. This informal consultation required Interior to prepare a biological assessment for the proposed activities, with which FWS concurred. FWS officials told us that both its formal and informal consultations included conservation recommendations for Interior intended to further minimize the potential for adverse effects of proposed actions on listed species and critical habitat or further a species recovery. FWS officials explained that, again, similar to NOAA, by providing input informally through the NEPA process and the ESA Section 7 consultations, it has ensured that Interior's final Gulf of Mexico multilease sale EIS and ESA consultation documents have included the necessary conservation measures—such as Notices to Lessees and Operators or lease stipulations—to protect threatened or endangered species under its jurisdiction. Accordingly, all subsequent authorization of oil and gas activities, including approvals of exploration and development plans or drilling permits, would be tiered back to the relevant Gulf of Mexico multilease sale EIS and ESA biological opinion or biological assessment. As a result, as oil and gas development moves through Interior's postlease process—including the exploration and development plan and drilling permit review and approvals—FWS officials told us that they typically do not request or receive these documents from Interior and therefore do not typically comment on them as it relates to their authority under the ESA. Again, as with NOAA, the exception is if new information becomes available during the time period for which the biological opinion is in effect, such as with the *Deepwater Horizon* incident, in which case Interior is required to reinitiate Section 7 ESA consultations. On July 30, 2010, Interior requested reinitiation of Section 7 ESA consultation with FWS. Subsequent to the *Deepwater Horizon* incident, on July 30, 2010, Interior requested reinitiation of Section 7 consultation with FWS. However, FWS did not reinitiate consultation at this time because no assessments of the current status of listed species as a result of the oil spill has been made available to FWS to serve as a basis for assessing the effects of the proposed actions. In the interim, Interior has determined that the existing September 14, 2007, biological assessment remains in effect.

State Government Stakeholders

State government stakeholders provided input to Interior through commenting on Gulf of Mexico multilease sale EIS and other lease sale EIS documents and consistency reviews conducted under the Coastal Zone Management Act.

National Environmental Policy Act. Of the five state agencies from Gulf of Mexico states that we reviewed, only the Mississippi Department of

Appendix III: Federal and State Stakeholder
Input to Interior's Proposed Gulf of Mexico Oil
and Gas Activities for 2002 through 2012

Marine Resources did not comment on any of Interior's Gulf of Mexico multilease sale EIS documents or individual lease sale EIS documents from approximately 2002 through January 2012. Of the remaining four state agencies that provided comments, Louisiana's Department of Natural Resources was most consistent in commenting on Interior's draft lease sale EIS documents, commenting on five of the six included in our analysis period (see table 9).

Table 9: State's Input to Interior's Gulf of Mexico OCS Lease Sale EIS NEPA documents, 2002-2012

	Alabama Department of Environmental Management	Florida Department of Environmental Protection	Louisiana Department of Natural Resources	Mississippi Department of Marine Resources	Texas General Land Office
Gulf of Mexico Lease Sale EIS Documents Prior to the *Deepwater Horizon* Incident					
Final Gulf of Mexico OCS 2003-2007 Multilease Sale EIS (November 2002)	Yes	No	Yes	No	No
Final Gulf of Mexico OCS Lease Sales 189 and 197 Eastern Planning Area EIS (May 2003)[a]	No	Yes	Yes	No	Yes
Final Gulf of Mexico OCS 2007 – 2012 Multilease Sale EIS (April 2007)	Yes	No	Yes	No	No
Final Gulf of Mexico OCS Lease Lease Sale 224 Eastern Planning Area Supplemental EIS (October 2007)[a]	No	No	No	No	No
Final Gulf of Mexico OCS Supplemental 2009 – 2012 Supplemental EIS (September 2008)[b]	Yes	No	No	No	No
Gulf of Mexico Lease Sale EIS Documents After the *Deepwater Horizon* Incident					
Final Gulf of Mexico OCS Lease Sale 218 Western Planning Area Supplemental EIS (August 2011)[c]	No	No	No	No	No
Final Gulf of Mexico OCS Lease Sale 216 and 222 Central Planning Area Supplemental EIS (January 2012)[c]	Yes	No	Yes	No	No

Source: GAO analysis of Interior and state documents and input from state officials.

[a]Due to the drilling moratorium in the eastern planning area of the Gulf of Mexico, Interior does not include lease sales that could affect the eastern planning area in its programmatic Gulf of Mexico multilease sale EIS documents; rather, it prepares a separate lease sale EIS.

[b]Interior had to supplement its programmatic Gulf of Mexico 2007-2012 multilease sale EIS because of the Gulf of Mexico Energy Security Act of 2006.

[c]Interior created a separate lease sale EIS due to potential changes in the baseline conditions that may have occurred since the *Deepwater Horizon* incident.

Appendix III: Federal and State Stakeholder
Input to Interior's Proposed Gulf of Mexico Oil
and Gas Activities for 2002 through 2012

Coastal Zone Management Act. State agency officials responsible for complying with CZMA from the five Gulf of Mexico states told us that no oil and gas activities proposed by Interior since 2000 have been found to be inconsistent with the states' coastal zone management plan. In accordance with CZMA, states are required to approve or deny consistency certification under the CZMA for Interior's oil and gas proposed activities, including for Interior's Gulf of Mexico multilease sale EIS, individual lease sale EA documents, and exploration and development plans. Unlike most other stakeholders, states receive and have the opportunity to review and disapprove an operator's exploration and development plan if they find the proposed plan to be inconsistent with the state's coastal zone management plan. However, officials from two of the five Gulf of Mexico states characterized their consistency reviews as cursory. Officials from one of these state agencies said they are checking the documents for form and not content, while an official from another state agency explained that the states' approvals were mostly through default—that is, by not disapproving the project within the specified time frame, the project was found to be consistent with the state's coastal zone management plan. An official from another state agency said that while state officials conduct consistency reviews, they provide their most substantive input to Interior during the NEPA process. We attempted to obtain data from the states and report on their consistency determinations but found that the data were not sufficiently reliable for the purposes of our analysis.

Appendix IV: Comments from the Department of the Interior

United States Department of the Interior

OFFICE OF THE SECRETARY
Washington, DC 20240

JUL 1 2 2012

Mr. Frank Rusco
Director, Natural Resources and Environment
Government Accountability Office
441 G Street, N.W.
Washington, D.C. 20548

Dear Mr. Rusco:

Thank you for providing us with the Government Accountability Office's (GAO's) draft report entitled, *Oil and Gas Management: Interior's Reorganization Complete but Challenges Remain in Implementing New Requirements* (GAO-12-423). The Department of the Interior (DOI or Department) shares GAO's interest in improving management and oversight of oil and gas development on the Outer Continental Shelf (OCS). As we discussed on June 25, 2012, we agree with most of the report recommendations. We also greatly appreciate GAO's consideration of the serious concerns we have about certain limitations in the report's findings and analysis. We welcome GAO's willingness to review the supplemental analysis related to processing times for plans and permits, which the Department provided on June 29, 2012. If addressed in the report, this supplemental analysis would mitigate some of these concerns. Per our discussions with you and your staff, we have enclosed this supplemental analysis, and respectfully request that it (Enclosure 1) be included in the report as part of the Department's response. We detail additional issues and concerns below.

The Department welcomes critical examination of how we are performing and is open to recommendations for how we might further improve our operations and better carry out our responsibilities as stewards of important resources on the OCS. We therefore appreciate the thoughtful review undertaken by GAO. We are nonetheless concerned about certain aspects of the draft report. Foremost, we are concerned that the draft report does not provide an up-to-date picture of the Department's progress in implementing reforms and employing efficient processes from the *Deepwater Horizon* event in April 2010 to the present. In some cases, the draft report draws upon data from a time period that ended <u>before</u> the *Deepwater Horizon* incident and institution of DOI's reforms. We recognize that GAO must select a discrete time period to review so that it may complete its analysis. We believe, however, that reviewing readily available data over a longer period of time would lead to a more accurate assessment of the progress the Department has made over the last two years to help ensure safe and environmentally responsible development of oil and gas on the OCS. Inclusion of this more representative data and analysis would strengthen the report significantly.

In addition to information on processing times for plans and permits addressed in Enclosure 1, we believe that a more robust description of other recent reviews, reforms, and improvements that DOI has undertaken would give the public, DOI stakeholders, and Congress a better sense of the current state of affairs with respect to development and regulation on the OCS. One area that we believe would benefit from further attention is the review of National Environmental Policy Act (NEPA) analysis for plan amendments. We are also concerned that the draft report does not reflect the breadth of the Department's efforts to reexamine and reform its programs, regulations, and information technology systems. Further, the draft report does not fully acknowledge the progress the Department has made on human capital issues.

We appreciate GAO's recognition that, following the *Deepwater Horizon* event, DOI implemented aggressive and sweeping reforms designed to raise drilling safety and environmental protection standards for oil and gas operations on the OCS. The Department's reforms also have substantially improved the evaluation of potential environmental effects of offshore oil and gas activity and emergency response preparedness. The Department also has successfully implemented substantive and organizational reforms that have significantly improved the management and oversight of energy operations on the OCS. These reforms include establishing three new, independent agencies, each with distinct and focused missions: the Bureau of Ocean Energy Management (BOEM), the Bureau of Safety and Environmental Enforcement (BSEE), and the Office of Natural Resources Revenue (ONRR).

While implementing improved safety, environmental, and evaluation standards, as well as organizational reforms, DOI has also implemented a robust stakeholder education program designed to explain new standards and procedures to industry. Frequent outreach to and communication with stakeholders across the spectrum of regulated industry; environmental groups; tribal, state, and local governments; and Federal agencies have been critical to our progress so far. These efforts will remain critical as we continue to pursue both increased rigor in oversight and improvements in regulatory efficiency.

We have also overseen a continuous improvement in the efficiency of the bureaus' regulatory and review processes. DOI has made substantial and, as highlighted briefly below, demonstrable progress in promoting industry compliance with the heightened standards. At the same time, we are refining the new bureaus' plan review and permitting processes to make them more rigorous, transparent, efficient, and predictable.

In developing and implementing this reform agenda, the Department has incorporated the findings and recommendations of a number of independent as well as internal reviews, including but not limited to—

- the report of the National Commission on the BP *Deepwater Horizon* Oil Spill and Offshore Drilling;
- the United States Coast Guard and DOI Joint Investigation Team report;
- the DOI Safety Oversight Board report;
- Secretary of the Navy Ray Mabus' report to the President; and
- the National Academy of Engineering report on the Macondo Well-*Deepwater Horizon* blowout.

2

We will continue to draw from and build upon the findings and recommendations of these reviews, as well as GAO's prior reviews and reports and the analysis and recommendations contained in this draft report.

As mentioned above, we also believe that the discussion in the report of BOEM's analyses of plan amendments under NEPA does not paint a representative picture of DOI's reform efforts since the *Deepwater Horizon* incident. The draft report considers only plan data through April 19, 2010—the day <u>before</u> the *Deepwater Horizon* blowout. Therefore, it does not consider important post-*Deepwater Horizon* reforms. For example, the report does not address the heightened standards BOEM has established regarding calculation of worst case discharge potential. The discussion also does not reflect BOEM's requirement—implemented in August 2010—that all deepwater exploration and development plans be subject to site-specific environmental assessments, rather than being categorically excluded from such reviews as was the practice prior to the *Deepwater Horizon* blowout.

The draft report also does not fully illustrate the scope and significance of DOI's accomplishments in strategically and comprehensively reexamining its leasing, planning, permitting, and inspection and enforcement programs; its foundational regulations; and its information technology systems. For example, BSEE's Strategic Plan is aligned to address GAO and other external report recommendation action areas. BSEE has also initiated an analysis of regulatory gaps as well as a comprehensive review of its inspection and enforcement program. Moreover, to ensure that policy and regulations are captured in the operation of information technology systems, DOI has initiated a review of the Technical Information Management System, including ePlans, eInspections, and ePermits. We have made significant progress, and our work continues in all of these areas. We appreciate that GAO's recommendations are generally consistent with and are supportive of these continuing efforts, but we believe recognition in the draft report of these efforts would create a more valid depiction of the reforms to date.

Finally, while the Department also agrees with GAO's concerns about the ongoing human capital issues surrounding offshore oil and gas management, the draft report in our view does not sufficiently acknowledge how the Department's efforts have resulted in an aggressive recruiting effort, using congressionally authorized special pay rates and retention strategies for key skills. The Department has taken steps to identify skill gaps and conducted a workload and workforce analysis for Gulf of Mexico operations. Additionally, BSEE has continued to refine its approach to training personnel to implement a consistent, progressive technical training program for offshore inspectors, engineers, and scientists—providing a clear path forward for continued technical development over their careers. BOEM is also participating in a pilot to implement DOI's Strategic Workforce Management Plan, which engages the bureau in detailed workforce planning using a standardized model.

The Department is committed to effectively managing offshore Federal oil and gas to the full extent of our authority and resources. Our objective—in Secretary of the Interior Ken Salazar's words—is to achieve the "gold standard" and world leadership in the management of offshore resources, operational safety, and environmental compliance. We appreciate your cooperation in working on this draft report as we strive to achieve these very important goals.

3

We have enclosed for your consideration, in addition to the supplemental analysis, some technical comments on the draft report (Enclosure 2). If you have any questions, please contact Andrea Nygren, BOEM Audit Liaison Officer, at 202-208-4343, or John Keith, BSEE, Chief of Policy and Analysis, at 202-208-3236.

Sincerely yours,

Marcilynn A. Burke
Acting Assistant Secretary
Land and Minerals Management

Enclosures
  1 – Additional Plans and Permits Data for GAO 12-423 (6 pp)
  2 – Technical Comments GAO-12-423 (9 pp)

4

ENCLOSURE 1

DOI Additional Plans and Permits Data for
Government Accountability Office (GAO) Draft Report

*Oil and Gas Management: Interior's Reorganization Complete
but Challenges Remain in Implementing New Requirements (GAO-12-423)*

Many of the most significant findings in the draft report—particularly with respect to the nature and timing of plan and permit reviews—could be buttressed by analysis of information and statistics from broader time periods. For example, the draft report's findings and analysis draw largely upon data from a period concluding as of September 30, 2011, before the reorganization into the three bureaus was completed. Thus, while in some cases the draft report focuses on the period following the blowout, that was also the period when reforms and improvements were only in the early stages of planning and implementation.

As shown in Figures 1 and 2 below, processing times have significantly decreased since the period immediately following the *Deepwater Horizon* event. They currently average 30-60 days for deepwater permits, and less than 100 days for deepwater plans. These data are accessible on the bureaus' websites.

<u>Plans</u>

**Days to Approve Deepwater Exploration Plans and Development Plans
Requiring Environmental Assessments
Submitted After 9/22/2010, Approved Before 5/30/2012**

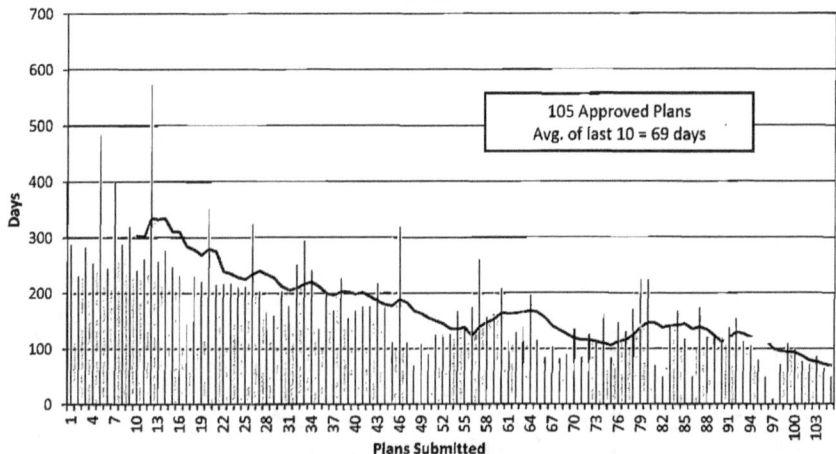

Figure 1. Graph of plan approval times for deepwater exploration plans and development plans (DOCDs) after September 22, 2010, and approved before May 30, 2012. The earliest submitted plans are on the left; more recently submitted plans are on the right. The trend line in this chart is a moving average of the 10 previous plan approval times, designed to highlight the longer-term trends. The total number of plans = 105; the average approval time for the 10 most recently approved plans prior to 5/30/2012 is 69 days.

Enclosure 1-1

The tables below reflect revisions to the draft report's analysis on plans Tables 1 (p. 35) and 2 (p. 36). There are two differences between the data in the tables below and the GAO's analysis:

1. GAO considered only those plans that were both submitted and approved in the same timeframe. BOEM believes this unnecessarily limits the number of plans considered, and thus as GAO notes, makes the data for the more recent time periods too limited a basis upon which to draw a firm conclusion. In the tables below, we included broader sets of data. For shallow water plans, the tables provide information for plans submitted after June 8, 2010, and approved by May 31, 2012. For deepwater plans, the tables provide information for plans submitted after October 12, 2010, and approved by May 31, 2012.

2. BOEM added plans approved through May 31, 2012, to include the more up-to-date information. BOEM did not change GAO's data for the January 2000 through April 2010 period.

GAO's general conclusion remains valid: "in some cases, review times and numbers of amendments per approved plan have recently decreased, although not to levels prior to the *Deepwater Horizon* incident" (page 32, second full paragraph, second sentence). The data shows that, while the number of plans submitted and approved is growing, the approval times are decreasing for all categories of plans. However, with the greater number of plans and additional time period considered, BOEM believes these conclusions can be made without characterizing them as "provisional." The fact that these approval times are not as short as prior to the *Deepwater Horizon* blowout and oil spill is not surprising. A number of new requirements and reforms result in longer processing times for plans. These changes include new requirements for more detailed information from operators about worst case discharge and blowout scenarios, along with information about how they would respond to a blowout and the new policy directing that all deepwater drilling plans be analyzed in Environmental Assessments instead of categorical exclusion reviews. However, BOEM views these changes as important to ensuring that operators are held to higher environmental standards, and that the projects receive an appropriate level of NEPA review.

Table 1: Deepwater Exploration and Development Plans Review Time Frames and Number of Amendments for Approved Deepwater Exploration and Development Plans

	Deepwater Plans					
	Exploration			Development		
	January 1, 2000, through April 19, 2010	October 12, 2010, through May 31, 2011	June 1, 2011, through May 31, 2012	January 1, 2000, through April 19, 2010	October 12, 2010, through May 31, 2011	June 1, 2011, through May 31, 2012
Total number of approved plans	1,374	50	66	448	32	39
Median days from initial plan submission to the plan approved date	38	122	73.5	57	121.5	79
Average number of amendments per approved plan	0.63	6.22	3.51	0.79	4.16	2.82

Note: Table includes plans submitted in the designated time period and approved no later than May 31, 2012.

Enclosure 1-2

Table 2: Shallow Water Exploration and Development Plans Review Time Frames and Number of Amendments for Approved Deepwater Exploration and Development Plans

	Shallow water Plans					
	Exploration			Development		
	January 1 2000, through April 19, 2010	June 8, 2010 through May 31, 2011	June 1, 2011 through May 31, 2012	January 1 2000, through April 19, 2010	June 8, 2010 through May 31, 2011	June 1, 2011 through May 31, 2012
Total number of approved plans	1,982	25	27	2,579	73	213
Median days from initial plan submission to the plan approved date	39	109	67	43	99.5	45
Average number of amendments per approved plan	0.54	4.76	3.81	0.47	3.68	1.93

Note: Table includes plans submitted in the designated time period and approved no later than May 31, 2012.

Permits

Days to Approve Deepwater New Well Permits Submitted After 10/12/2010, Approved Before 5/31/2012

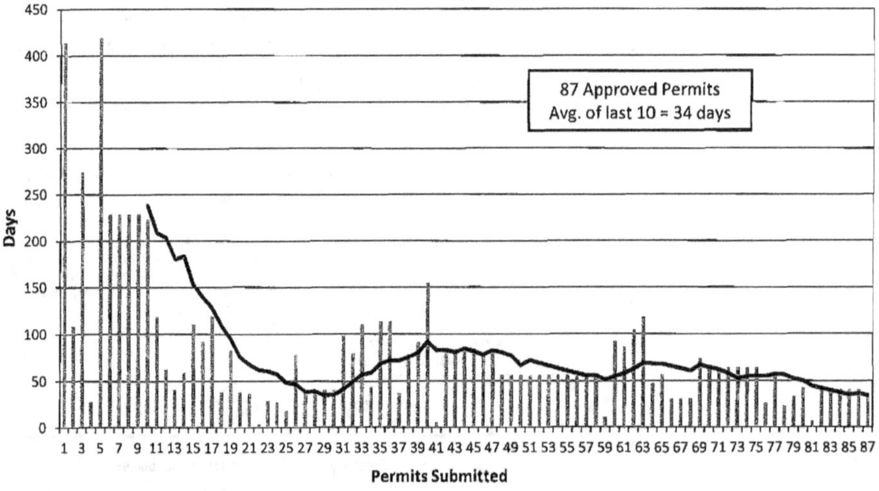

Figure 2. Graph of permit approval times for deepwater New Well permits submitted after October 12, 2010, and approved before May 31, 2012. The earliest submitted permits are on the left; more recently submitted permits are on the right. The trend line in this chart is a moving average of the 10 previous permit approval times, designed to highlight the longer-term trends. The total number of permits = 87; the average approval time for the 10 most recently approved permits prior to 5/31/2012 is 34 days.

Enclosure 1-3

. . .

The tables below reflect revisions to the draft report's analysis on permits in Tables 3 (p. 43) and 4 (p. 44). There are two differences between the data in the tables below and the GAO's analysis:

1. For shallow water permits, the tables provide information for permits submitted after June 8, 2010, and approved by May 31, 2012. For deepwater permits, the tables provide information for permits submitted after October 12, 2010, and approved by May 31, 2012.

2. BSEE added permits approved through May 31, 2012, to include more up-to-date information. There is no change to GAO's data for the January 2000 through April 2010 period.

BSEE agrees with the general conclusions that GAO draws from the data regarding permit review times: the time to review permits increased immediately after the new safety requirements were instituted, but those times shortened significantly as operators and BSEE staff became more familiar with those new requirements. However, the use of GAO selected end points for the two post-*Deepwater Horizon* time windows in Tables 3 and 4, coupled with the requirement that permits be submitted and approved in each of those windows in order to be included in the analysis, results in a sample size that is too small to identify trends.

BSEE believes an alternative methodology using the exact same data used by GAO for Table 3 would provide a much more comprehensive picture of both the actual time it takes to review permits and the trend since the *Deepwater Horizon*. For example, in Table 3 GAO reports 2 total deepwater New Well permits submitted and approved between October 12, 2010, and May 31, 2011, with a median approval time of 68 days. This analysis does not include another 15 permits that were submitted in that timeframe and later approved. The situation is similar in the June 1, 2011 – September 30, 2011 time window. If the approval time is displayed graphically for all permits submitted after October 12, 2010, and approved by May 31, 2012, a plot that clearly shows the trends in approval time can be generated (Figure 2).

Enclosure 1-4

Table 3: Review Time Frames and Average Number of Returns Per Submission for All Types of Approved Deepwater Drilling Permits

	New well			Revised new well		
	January 1, 2005, through April 19, 2010	October 12, 2010, through May 31, 2011	June 1, 2011, through May 31, 2012	January 1, 2005, through April 19, 2010	October 12, 2010, through May 31, 2011	June 1, 2011, through May 31, 2012
Number of submittals	414	17	70	687	35	192
Median days from initial submittal until final approval	20	119	56	1	3.8	2.1
Average number of returned drilling permits per approved submittal	1.57	3.5	2.04	0.54	1.69	0.44

	Sidetrack			Revised sidetrack		
	January 1, 2005, through April 19, 2010	October 12, 2010, through May 31, 2011	June 1, 2011, through May 31, 2012	January 1, 2005, through April 19, 2010	October 12, 2010, through May 31, 2011	June 1, 2011, through May 31, 2012
Number of submittals	259	7	21	177	15	45
Median days from initial submittal until final approval	4	34	10.6	1	1.7	1.3
Average number of returned drilling permits per approved submittal	0.85	3.88	1.81	0.32	1.00	0.48

	Bypass			Revised bypass		
	January 1, 2005, through April 19, 2010	October 12, 2010, through May 31, 2011	June 1, 2011, through May 31, 2012	January 1, 2005, through April 19, 2010	October 12, 2010, through May 31, 2011	June 1, 2011, through May 31, 2012
Number of submittals	149	7	28	124	10	40
Median days from initial submittal until final approval	1	0.7	1.8	1	2.9	2
Average number of returned drilling permits per approved submittal	0.55	2.29	0.79	0.39	1.00	0.73

Enclosure 1-5

Table 4: Review Time Frames and Average Number of Returns per Submission for all Types of Approved Shallow Water Drilling Permits

	New well			Revised new well		
	January 1, 2005, through April 19, 2010	June 8, 2010, through May 31, 2011	June 1, 2011, through May 31, 2012	January 1, 2005, through April 19, 2010	June 8, 2010, through May 31, 2011	June 1, 2011, through May 31, 2012
Number of submittals	1,105	51	67	1,246	93	96
Median days from initial submittal until final approval	11	38	29	1	1.7	1.2
Average number of returned drilling permits per approved submittal	1.25	2.72	1.97	0.31	0.85	0.72

	Sidetrack			Revised sidetrack		
	January 1, 2005, through April 19, 2010	June 8, 2010, through May 31, 2011	June 1, 2011, through May 31, 2012	January 1, 2005, through April 19, 2010	June 8, 2010, through May 31, 2011	June 1, 2011, through May 31, 2012
Number of submittals	648	81	79	492	94	83
Median days from initial submittal until final approval	4	23	18.6	1	1	1.6
Average number of returned drilling permits per approved submittal	0.72	2.20	1.64	0.34	0.75	0.63

	Bypass			Revised bypass		
	January 1, 2005, through April 19, 2010	June 8, 2010, through May 31, 2011	June 1, 2011, through May 31, 2012	January 1, 2005, through April 19, 2010	June 8, 2010, through May 31, 2011	June 1, 2011, through May 31, 2012
Number of submittals	377	20	45	233	14	41
Median days from initial submittal until final approval	1	1	1	1	0.9	1
Average number of returned drilling permits per approved submittal	0.38	1.14	0.87	0.26	0.38	0.60

Enclosure I-6

Appendix V: GAO Contact and Staff Acknowledgments

GAO Contact	Frank Rusco, (202) 512-3841 or ruscof@gao.gov
Staff Acknowledgments	In addition to the contact named above, Christine Kehr, Assistant Director; Nirmal Chaudhary; Glenn C. Fischer; Cindy Gilbert; David Greyer; Michael Kendix; Alison O'Neill; Kiki Theodoropoulos; Barbara Timmerman; and Nick Weeks made key contributions to this report.